A FORK IN THE ROAD

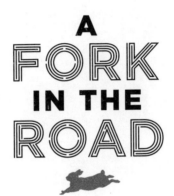

lonely planet

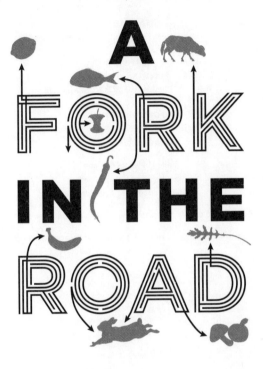

A FORK IN THE ROAD

TALES OF FOOD, PLEASURE & DISCOVERY ON THE ROAD

EDITED BY
JAMES OSELAND

LONELY PLANET PUBLICATIONS
Melbourne • Oakland • London

A FORK IN THE ROAD

Tales of Food, Pleasure & Discovery on the Road

Published by
Lonely Planet Publications

HEAD OFFICE

90 Maribyrnong Street, Footscray, Victoria, 3011, Australia

BRANCHES

150 Linden Street, Oakland CA 94607, USA
201 Wood Ln, London, W12 7TQ, United Kingdom

PUBLISHED 2013

Printed by Hang Tai Printing Company, Hong Kong
Printed in China

Edited by James Oseland
Cover design by Roberto Devicq
Design and layout by Leon Mackie

National Library of Australia Cataloguing-in-Publication entry

A Fork in the Road: Tales of Food, Pleasure & Discovery on the Road
Edited by James Oseland

1st Editon

978 1 74321 844 0 (pbk.)

Voyages and travels.
Travelers' writings.

Oseland, James

808.8032

Paper in this book is certified against the Forest Stewardship Council™ standards. FSC™ promotes environmentally responsible, socially beneficial and economically viable management of the world's forests.

JAMES OSELAND

James is the editor-in-chief of *Saveur*, America's most critically acclaimed food magazine. Under his editorship, the magazine has won more than 40 awards, including numerous James Beard journalism awards, and three from the American Society of Magazine Editors. His 2006 book, *Cradle of Flavor*, a memoir with recipes about his time living in Southeast Asia, was named one of the best books of that year by *Time Asia*, *The New York Times*, and *Good Morning America* and won awards from the James Beard Foundation and the International Association of Culinary Professionals. He is also the editor of *Saveur*'s cookbooks, including *Saveur: The New Comfort Food* and *Saveur: The Way We Cook*. James is a judge on the cooking competition program *Top Chef Masters*, and appears as a guest on other international television shows. He is writing *Jimmy Neurosis*, a memoir of his punk rock youth in the 1970s, for Ecco Press, a HarperCollins imprint. James has lived in India and Indonesia and now resides in New York City with his husband, Daniel.

CONTENTS

INTRODUCTION

James Oseland

E very traveler has two or three or even a hundred of
them: moments on a journey when you taste something
and you're forever changed. It might be a fancy or dazzling
dish served by a tuxedoed waiter, or it might simply be
an unexpected flavor or unfamiliar ingredient, offered by
strangers and encountered by happenstance. At their most
intense, these tastes of the new reveal something elemental
about the place you're in, and about yourself. These are
the kinds of experiences I asked the writers in this book to
capture in their stories.

One of my earliest such epiphanies happened when I was
twelve. My father took me to a restaurant in Chicago called
Jacques, one of the great American temples of French cuisine
in the postwar era, a kind of place that doesn't exist much
anymore. Though we were only an hour from our suburban
home, this elegant redoubt in Chicago's downtown Loop

felt like another planet. Dad told me that Jacques was one of the best restaurants in the country. I don't know if that was true, but the duck à l'orange I had there certainly transformed me. The limpid and tangy sauce, the rich and fatty meat, the mingling of sweet and savory flavors—it was too magnificent for words. My enjoyment of the dish, which I'd ordered at Dad's suggestion, seemed to draw me closer to this taciturn man who'd always been a mystery to me. More than that, it made me feel, for the first time, like an adult. Or at least it gave me a taste of what being grown up might feel like.

Another moment of transformation through food happened seven years later, on my first solo trip abroad, to Southeast Asia. One stormy night, on a visit to Penang, Malaysia, I stumbled upon a night market in the middle of a field on the edge of town. While wandering through the warren of food stalls, in the center of which a Chinese opera troupe was performing, I met an old man who spoke a little English. He took me around to all the vendors, pointing out the foods each of them was selling. I sampled nearly everything, but what I remember more vividly than almost any dish I've eaten since is the *char kuey teow*, a Malaysian street-food staple of stir-fried rice noodles. I was blown away by the new flavors: the briny taste of fresh-caught cockles, the bite of Chinese spring onions, the hot, spiky funk of chile sambal, and the deep savor that I later learned can only come from ingredients that have been stir-fried in pork fat over extreme heat. The food was literally life-changing. I felt I suddenly understood this place, and I realized with equal suddenness that I wasn't necessarily the person I thought I was up until that moment. I'd discovered another part of me. The depth and brightness of the flavors told of a world that was utterly different from what I'd known, and they told me I had a place in it.

Now I seek out that feeling of discovery wherever I happen to be eating. Even the lunch-hour meals I dash out for from my office in Manhattan can transport me, and put me in touch with something fascinating. A sortie to my favorite South Indian vegetarian place on Lexington Avenue or to my favorite Korean lunch counter on 32nd Street loosens the grip of the workday and lets me experience the world again in a purely sensory way. These humble meals tell me that there is always another epiphany around the corner. They remind me of the great, exciting promise of life.

There really is something fabulous and even miraculous about the act of eating. Savoring food is the one thing we do every day that is direct and unmediated. Taste does not lie. It's pure. The impressions it leaves are sharp, invigorating, and emotional. And those impressions can last a lifetime.

That's what I find so beautiful about the essays in this book. Each of them says something ineffable about how we process and remember tastes and sensations, and about how they alter our view of the world. The stories encompass a vast mosaic of experience, from bitter to sweet to everything in between, and an equally vast range of voices. Some are rough, some are intensely refined. But they all have one thing in common: they chronicle food and eating in a deeply personal way.

Each story will take you on a journey, whether it's restaurant critic Gael Greene supping on star fruit in the Peruvian jungle, novelist Francine Prose coaxing a cassoulet from the kitchen of two bickering restaurateurs in rural France, or chef Martin Yan watching his mother at the stove when he was a child in Guangzhou (a wholly transporting experience that didn't involve leaving home). But the essays in this book offer more than armchair travel. They will arouse your appetite for life-changing moments of your own. They will prompt you to seek your own fork in the road.

GILES COREN is the award-winning restaurant critic of *The Times* of London, to which he also contributes a weekly opinion column. He is editor-at-large of *Esquire*'s U.K. edition, is the author of the nonfiction books *How to Eat Out, Anger Management for Beginners*, and a novel, *Winkler*, and has presented numerous television series for the BBC.

CONSIDER THE TWINKIE

Giles Coren

In the late 1970s, when great cairns of bin bags piled high on every London street corner, when the kitchen lights flickered and died each dinnertime (at first excitingly, then increasingly less so), when the grown-ups wore brown and smelled of Rothmans and Maxwell House, and I wore little grey flannel shorts and a pink school cap, my waking and my night-time dreams were of escape. And like so many of the miserable and dispossessed before me, the badly treated and the badly fed, the bored, the lonely and the small, the place to which I dreamed of escaping was America.

And also like so many other would-be emigrants from dark and dismal lands, I focused much of my longing upon food. Just as the Israelites followed Moses to Canaan largely for the jumbo portions of keenly priced milk and honey he promised were on offer there, so I longed for the brightly coloured and endlessly thrilling mouthfuls that were eaten on American TV shows and in the American books and comics that I devoured nightly, after a supper of thin, brown fish fingers, all grey in the middle, with brown tinned peas, followed by a tooth-aching brick of Wall's non-dairy ice cream, tasting of frozen margarine and Hermesetas.

In America, they had Coca-Cola, Dr Pepper, Lucky Charms, Cheerios and Big Macs from McDonald's. In Callaghan and Healey's Britain, we had Panda cola, Vimto, Tizer, Shredded Wheat, Puffa Puffa Rice, Birds Eye frozen beef burgers (oh, that sad, grey, ashen taste of bovine mortuary slab) and Wimpy bars.

Sure, some of the American versions just about existed here by the time I was ten years old, but they were not ubiquitous, and as far as the grown-ups were concerned, who grew up with rationing, made dinnertime more of a moral than a nutritional exercise ('Elbows off the table; don't talk with your mouth full; no getting down without permission …'), and gave us to believe that we were lucky to be eating at all, there was no question of travelling the extra miles across town, or spending the extra pence, that might occasionally have scored us the bona fide twentieth-century American originals we craved.

And some products you could not get here at all: applejacks, Hershey bars, Oreo biscuits, but most of all Hostess Twinkies.

Ah, Hostess Twinkies. The tastiest thing I never ate. These I knew about from comics, specifically the American DC comics I bought secondhand for 6p a throw because that four pence off the new price could be spent on 1p cola chews, with their slow-dissolving chemical tang of the New World, to be chewed while I read about Superman and Batman, Flash, Green Lantern … in adventures which stopped every three or five pages for adverts featuring full-page mini-adventures in which those very superheroes battled crime with the help of Hostess Twinkies, Hostess Cup Cakes or Hostess Fruit Pies (available in apple, cherry or blueberry flavour).

These confections seemed to me every bit as mythical as the magical flying foreigners who touted them, and indeed the very land from which they came. To say nothing of all the non-comestible pleasures my comics advertised, such as BB guns, X-ray specs (for looking at naked ladies THROUGH their clothes!), and colonies of real living sea creatures who would arrive by post, come alive in a tank of water and obey your every command.

All these items could be yours, the adverts promised, for a few cents and the provision of a zip code.

'Daaaaaaaad, what's a zip code?'

'It's like a postcode, but in America.'

'So what's our zip code?'

'We don't have a zip code. We only have a postcode.'

'Well, then how am I going to get a gun, some X-ray specs and a colony of mermaid slave girls?'

So my father explained to me about advertising. And when he had finished, I had only one question: 'When can we go to America?'

'One day?'

'When?'

15

'When you're older.'

'When?'

'Soon.'

'When.'

'Unless you shut up, never.'

'But Daaaaaad, you went to America.'

'Yes, son, I did. But not until I was twenty-three and …'

Then his eyes glazed over, and he was back in 1961, at the University of Minnesota, eating steaks the size of baseball mitts and three cheeseburgers at a time, queuing up over and over again at the college canteen, where they laid on this food mostly for the football players—a bounty that was unimaginable to a boy from Southgate, North London, who had grown up under wartime and post-war rationing, with hardly any meat or chocolate or eggs, living on soups made from the ninth boiling of a stoat. He talked about the food of his American sojourn endlessly. Later, when I wanted to ask about sex and drugs and rock and roll on American campuses in the 1960s (he also went to Yale and Berkeley), all he could talk about was the food.

And it was he who got me into cowboys, with their endless bacon and beans, eaten on laps off metal plates round a campfire, with a cup of coffee whose grounds they flung into the flames before rolling over and going to sleep. Such loucheness, such a casual approach to food … in my house no food was ever consumed anywhere but at the kitchen or dining-room tables, and nothing was ever, ever thrown anywhere. God, how I wanted to go to America.

Then one Christmas, 1980 I think it was, because John

Lennon had just been shot dead in New York, making me, for some reason, want to go to America even more, there was a card in my stocking from Santa Claus that read: 'Voucher: Valid for one trip to Disneyworld, leaving January 4th, also valid for parents and sister.'

Disneyworld. In Florida. In America.

And so, twenty-five years before I boarded planes to eat at El Bulli, the French Laundry, Chez Panisse, Noma and Arzak, I flew to America to eat EVERYTHING.

⟶⟶

On the final page of *The Great Gatsby* (my father's favourite book, and thus mine, and no small factor in my lifelong yearning for America), Nick Carraway wanders down to the beach and looks across at the American mainland from Long Island:

> And as the moon rose higher the inessential houses began to melt away until gradually I became aware of the old island here that flowered once for Dutch sailors' eyes—a fresh, green breast of the new world ... for a transitory enchanted moment man must have held his breath in the presence of this continent, compelled into an aesthetic contemplation he neither understood nor desired, face to face for the last time in history with something commensurate to his capacity for wonder.

And I knew just how those sailors felt as I pressed my ten-year-old face up hard against the cold plastic of the cabin window after eight or nine sleepless hours, and spied, looming up out of the wet gloaming as we descended into Miami airport, suspended high above a huge parking lot … the golden arches of McDonald's.

'Dad, can we go to McDonald's?'

'Yes.'

'But, Daaaaaaad! You promised … wait, did you say "Yes"?'

Oh frabjous day. Oh brave New World that has the power to make my father say yes to McDonald's. He never said yes to it at Shepherd's Bush Roundabout ahead of a two-hour drive to the New Forest, because of the smell it would make in the car. Or to the one in Golders Green, because there were no tables there, and he didn't like to eat while standing. Or to the one on Finchley Road because … I forget why not. But in America, clearly, everything was possible. Just like everyone had always said.

Maybe it was because in America, to eat in McDonald's is not a dim, cheap, dirty alternative to the authentic food of the host land. There, McDonald's is authentic. It is native. It is natural. It is real. And anyway, nobody in America has any table manners, so who cares if the kids eat with their hands and drink fizzy pop through a straw?

Oh, the daze in which I queued through immigration, picked up luggage, waited for cabs to be hailed, climbed in, pointed when I saw it, and ran, ran, ran out into the rain …

'Won't it be closed?' asked my mother. 'It's quarter past nine.'

'Closed?' I called back as I pushed open the door. 'Nothing closes in America. Not even at midnight!'

God, I remember the big pink face of the girl who took my order—I even think I remember that she was called Dana—and her thick, syrupy accent, and her failure at first to understand mine. And I remember the warmth of the fresh new burger in the beige polystyrene box (I miss those boxes: like tea in bone china, a Big Mac is most advantageously served on polystyrene—these new papery ones just won't do, they don't insulate the food properly, they allow it to cool and they lend it a mulchy, cellulose taste that I find cloying) and I remember the heat and steam as I popped it open and the nutty whiff of sesame; the softness as my teeth sank in to the point where childish incisor cracked the toasted surface and sank through air and bleached flour and a little bit of gypsum; then shredded lettuce, diced onion, crinkle-sliced pickled cucumber with that tell-tale whiff of dill (even now, the merest suggestion of dill in, say, a sauce for gravlax, just screams 'Big Mac!' at me); then 'special sauce', sweet, tangy, ever-so-slightly petrolly; then cheese, sort of, tacky if properly melted, no dairy flavours at all, but a pervasive umami that binds all the elements together; then meat, grey-black, sweaty … and there, as ever, the sadness began to set in.

After the first sugar rush, the descent. The post–Big Mac tristesse which becomes almost a wave of grief as you chew the last cold mouthful and toss the empty, ridiculously light box into the flapping bin at the door, and experience once again that aftermath of the triumph of expectation over reality.

And then jetlag sleep for what felt like days.

After that, everything began to look up. To begin with, we had scored from McDonald's (my baby sister and I) little

19

plastic figurines of Ronald McDonald and a character called the Hamburglar and a purple thing called Grimace that were as yet unknown in Britain and would ensure copious kudos points back home. Not to mention the opportunity to report that Big Macs here tasted very slightly different. Only very slightly, but enough to be noticed by a ten-year-old's hypersensitive virgin palate. And as Vincent Vega says, 'It's the little differences … I mean, they got the same shit over there that we got here, but it's just … it's just, there it's a little different.'

For example, the Raisin Bran which room service sent up on our first morning in the Orlando motel where we were staying: my mum and dad in one room, my sister and me in the other, alone with a phone and our first ever American room service menu.

Back home, we had Sultana Bran. It was my favourite cereal, but it was not without its failings. For the flakes were much thicker and harder in Sultana Bran than they were in Bran Flakes, for no reason I could ever ascertain, less malty, less inclined to mulch nicely with the delicious cold, silver-top milk the Unigate man brought every morning in tall glass bottles. And sultanas were all very well, but they were not as sweet and rich and treacly as raisins. Why did nobody see this apart from me?

Except someone did. The whole of America did! Oh, what a cereal this was: genuine Bran Flakes with tarry black raisins, not over-baked multi-grain crossover flakes with shrivelled green grapes. No wonder Superman and Batman chose to live here and not in shitty old England.

And then after the cereal, waffles. And pancakes. Not lame-o flat floury pancakes like on Shrove Tuesday but thick fluffy pancakes, with maple syrup and crispy bacon. Here, bacon was not piggy and wet and bendy but properly crisped, to a point where it was commensurate with man's capacity for wonder. And you were allowed syrup on it. Crispy bacon with maple syrup. Pudding at the same time as your main. Sweetness and savoury together. No waiting required. Where was the moral lesson in that?

Exactly. Nowhere. In America, you just ate whatever you wanted to, whenever you wanted to. And nobody had a word to say about it. So we ordered hamburgers to the room, with Coca-Cola, in the middle of the night. And chips. And ate them. And nothing bad happened to us. Once, we even asked for Vimto to see what the telephone guy would say. He said he would do his best to find something like it. Could we please describe it to him? But we couldn't. Who could? All we could do was giggle.

And when we couldn't wait for room service, we ran out into the corridor and bought food from the vending machine by the lifts. Food from a machine! The thing I remember best from there is Cheetos—slightly disappointing compared to a Wotsit, but exotic too, in their slight grittiness, toasty corn notes and bland, less insistent cheesiness.

And while we ate, we watched Heckle and Jeckle, Mighty Mouse, and a giant talking moose called Bullwinkle. Not Andy bloody black-and-white rubbishy Pandy or some stupid mule, like back in England. And then we went down to the lobby and played 'Asteroids', pinging the crap out of polygonal aggressors from a little magically swivelling triangle and trying to remember to hit 'hyperspace' whenever things got too hot.

In the end, I hardly recall if we ever got to Disneyworld. I suppose we must have done. But I remember nothing of it at all. What stayed with me forever were the hamburgers and the Raisin Bran, the machine-vended midnight snacks and the pancakes, the bacon and the maple syrup and the …

… wait! Oh no. I forgot to eat a Hostess Twinkie. That was the whole point of going to America: to sample whatever the hell this 'angel food cake' was, that was so delicious a legion of costumed superheroes swore by it.

Gradually, as I grew older and left comics behind, I forgot about Hostess Twinkies. And then last year, at the age of forty-two, I found myself in Los Angeles, filming a TV pilot for BBC America and desperate for a smackerel of something round about teatime o'clock. So in a break to reset cameras, I ducked into a small general store and was walking down the line of snack options, mulling over the various horrible pies and hideous granola bars, when I came upon a packet of Hostess Twinkies.

I stopped dead and looked around me. Was I really here? Was I really, finally about to eat one of these things? I looked at the packet and saw no natural ingredients at all. Through the polythene, the two bright yellow food fingers squished under my finger and thumb and then regained their shape like bath sponges. They were not refrigerated because a Twinkie, famously, will last for a hundred years, because it contains no unstabilised dairy proteins.

'You can't eat Twinkies!' yodelled a producer who had wandered in for cigarettes. 'Those things are gross, nobody eats those.'

And I was about to put them back, when a wormhole opened in the space–time continuum, and the little fellow in his shorts and cap from 1978 was standing there, desperate to know what a Twinkie tasted like, before getting back to his dreams of BB guns and X-ray specs. So I bought the packet, took it out into the California sunshine, and opened it.

I smelled it. It smelled of nothing at all. I bit in and looked down at the remaining chunk in my hand, a spongy, cylindrical yellow-orange carapace around a column of slick, shiny, white cream.

I bit. The carapace yielded like rotten flesh and moved across my palate like old wet carpet, the filling began to coat my gums like some sort of dermatological ointment, there was a mild whine of sugar and a mutter of 'cheese' from far, far away. Saliva rushed to the front of my mouth, summoned by hysterical, traumatised tastebuds. My tongue caught in my throat. My uvula trembled. My stomach heaved …

This, without question—and bollocks to Batman—was the most disgusting thing I had ever, ever eaten. Ever. In all my born days.

Apart, perhaps, from a Birds Eye beef burger.

FRANCINE PROSE is the author of more than 20 books of fiction and nonfiction. A Distinguished Visiting Writer at Bard College, she is the recipient of a James Beard Award for an essay she contributed to *Saveur* magazine.

WE'LL HAVE THE CASSOULET

Francine Prose

Everyone knows that the holidays can turn up the heat under simmering family tensions and cause them to boil over—sometimes with volcanic results. But for some reason I'd never expected to experience that sort of domestic eruption in a foreign country, involving someone else's family, a mini-disaster that exploded beyond the domestic dinner table to consume a restaurant kitchen.

I'd gone with my husband, our two sons, and my mother to spend Christmas in the south of France. This was in the early 1990s; my sons were entering adolescence. We'd planned to take part in all the elegant (the multicourse Christmas Eve dinner with its traditional thirteen desserts) and the funky, folkloric: the midnight mass, complete with sheep, at the church in Les Baux-de-Provence. Customs with which the region celebrated the season.

French friends who summered in the area told us about a small town—the name escapes me now—not far from Les Baux. There was a Nativity pageant that local people and their kids put on, every Sunday afternoon in December, at the high school. Very simple, very touching, and for the moment undiscovered by the tourists and Parisians in mink coats who crowded the chapel for the midnight mass in Les Baux.

Better yet, there was a fabulous restaurant just across the street from the school, the kind of place that had already begun to disappear: small, family-run, unpretentious, not expensive, serving only a few marvelous, perfectly prepared dishes. In other words, the fantasy French small-town bistro. The kind of place where local families went after Sunday mass. We could go for lunch there before the Nativity play. No reservations needed. Who knew if they had a phone.

The restaurant was exactly where—and the way—our friends had described. When we got there, the owner and his wife were serving early lunch to a few multi-generational French families who did in fact look as if they'd come from mass.

A simple place, nothing fancy. But someone obviously cared about the details: the dishes, the cutlery, the linen. It smelled like garlic and olive oil. Delicious. We were overjoyed.

The drive there had taken longer than we'd thought, and we were all hungry. And when you travel with kids, even older kids, it's hard to *relax* when they're hungry. Everybody just be patient!

The middle-aged owner (moustache, plump, thinning hair, big smile) stepped straight out of a Marcel Pagnol film from the 1930s to greet us and showed us to a table. He apologized. He had things to do, and he disappeared into the kitchen.

A waitress (his wife, it seemed clear) brought us a basket of delicious bread and a dish of olives. She was blonde and looked like a Provençal country-western singer.

We studied the menu, which, as promised, was small and appealing, but large enough so that (this was my idea) we could all order different things and taste one another's food. We would only be there once, so why not have the full experience?

My sons said, 'Tripe? Disgusting.' We could have whatever we wanted. They were having the steak frites.

Fine, I said. Whatever. No one had to eat tripe.

When the waitress returned to take her orders, she kept glancing back at the kitchen.

⟶⟶⟶

I'm not sure I would have been so attuned to the signs of kitchen meltdown if I hadn't been around for a few in the past. Scenes were part of the drama at the cooking school near our house, where you could eat delicious French food and watch, behind a window, chefs reducing culinary students to tears.

The first wood-fired pizza place in our town in upstate New York was opened by two brothers, and the wife of one. On the first night they were in business, one brother hit the other over the head with a skillet and sent him to the emergency room.

After that it was just the one guy and his wife. They had a mural painted of themselves looking out on a Tuscan landscape. Until one night we went there and noticed that the husband had been painted out of the mural.

In any case, I felt something familiar in the air of the restaurant in Provence. A sort of sonic rumble. The calm before the you-know-what.

Maybe I was imagining it. I decided to think that I was.

We ordered soups and salads, then the veal stew, the roast duck, the goose. Two orders of steak frites. The waitress wrote down what we wanted, and, with a hasty glance at the kitchen, vanished through the swinging door.

Ten minutes passed, then twenty. The waitress brought more olives. So far, okay, it was fine. This was what you expected if you ate at places that hadn't yet discovered what a microwave could do to food.

Another five minutes, maybe more. One by one, the French families left. Were they looking at us that way because they knew something we didn't, or was it just that we were strangers and they were curious why we were there?

They all knew how long we'd been waiting. We asked, What's going on? They shrugged and smiled. We were strangers. If they knew anything, they didn't have to tell us.

The last French family had been gone for a few more minutes when we heard a man shouting, really loud, from the kitchen, phrases that were way beyond my college French. There was some thudding of things against walls, and breaking. Now the woman was yelling too. No one seemed to have been hurt.

We looked at each other. Now what?

The owner slammed through the doors so hard and fast he seemed to levitate slightly off the ground. He passed us without seeing us. He didn't care how long we'd waited. We were not his problem. The front door banged shut behind him. Facing the window, I watched him get into his car and drive off.

Probably we should have left. I don't know why we stayed. To see what would happen next, I guess. And also: we'd ordered lunch! I didn't remember seeing any other places to eat nearby. It was Sunday afternoon, it was starting to snow. The Nativity play was supposed to start in just over an hour. We were hungry!

A nervous young man I hadn't seen before opened the kitchen door and looked out. He saw us and seemed even more nervous than he'd been before. After a while the waitress reappeared. Her eye makeup was blurry, but otherwise she was okay. Obviously, she knew that we had heard and seen her husband leave. So it was an awkward moment.

She said she was sorry, they didn't have anything we'd ordered. Not the duck, not the veal, not the steak frites. *Rien du tout.*

My mother said, 'So okay, what *do* you have?' It struck me as the kind of question that, under the circumstances, only a sweet little old lady could get away with asking.

The waitress looked startled.

'Cassoulet,' she said.

'What's cassoulet?' asked our sons.

'Franks and beans,' we said. 'You'll like it.' They asked how I knew they'd like it. I said I knew.

'Fine,' I told the waitress. 'We'll have the cassoulet.'

'Ten minutes,' she said.

'We've got an hour until the play,' I said.

'Who cares about that?' said my mother.

⇢⇥⥲

Was it really a great cassoulet? The greatest cassoulet ever?
I remember that it was. I remember thinking that it made
sense the dish she had on hand, and could give us, was one of
those foods that got better, a day or a few days later.

Every bean was a masterpiece. The chunks of sausage
were sublime. I'd thought I'd known something about duck
confit, but until now I'd known nothing. I'd been a cassoulet
virgin. Our dishes were topped with a breadcrumb crust that
crumbled into the sauce from the beans.

Our sons ate it all. They loved it. My mother couldn't finish
hers, and divided what was left between her two growing
grandsons.

We asked for our bill. How reasonable! We paid. We
thanked the waitress a dozen times. My husband left a giant
tip, though we knew that a lot of French people didn't tip at all.

We got to the school auditorium in time to see the Nativity
play, which was sweet and touching. But by then I'd been
to years of school plays, and no matter how pretty the little
French angels were, how tender the little boy shepherds, I
couldn't stay interested for all that long in someone else's
kid's school play.

What we took away from the day was a renewed and
lifelong respect for cassoulet. The food of dependability. The
food of better-the-next-day, of even better the day after that.
The food of many flavors melding into one. The pops and

bursts of each mouthful of beans, the fattiness of the sausage and duck, the salty, dark, crumbly crust. The food of warmth on a winter's day. The food of Sunday afternoons. The food of: Your husband has just walked out the door, and there's nothing else in the kitchen.

Let me be clear about one thing. I would rather have spared the wife the unpleasantness of what had just happened. I would have skipped our fabulous cassoulet if the Sunday afternoon hadn't exploded. But we weren't the cause of it, we were just the witnesses, and in a way, I guess, its beneficiaries. We ate what was in the kitchen, and paid our bill and left.

Did the couple reconcile? Did they split up forever? Did he drive away and never come back, or did this happen every Sunday? Which possibility would have been worse?

I have no explanation, or any way of knowing. All I have is a partial memory of the human drama of that afternoon alongside a much more pleasant and ever so slightly guilty memory of the food.

SANDI TAN was born in Singapore, educated in the United Kingdom and at Columbia University, and lives in Pasadena, California. A former journalist and filmmaker, her debut novel *The Black Isle* was published in 2012. To find out more visit sanditan.com.

THE GOOD WITCH

Sandi Tan

On the day I was born, my father gave me up to his mother. I state this not to elicit pity or envy, but only to establish how I was torn between two cultures from the very beginning: father and grandmother (three, if counting my mother, but she was kept out of the picture). Duality had always informed me and so, too, adaptability: I would be equally uncomfortable everywhere.

My grandmother's house in leafy early-1980s Singapore was all custom Knoll replicas, deep-pile silk rugs, some books, servants. My father, in contrast, was an angry guy with a perm who drove his MG Roadster way too fast—no house, no books, no servants, and whenever he laughed it was most likely at his own fart jokes. His favorite word was 'bugger', used as a noun, never as a verb—*that's sick, man!*

Sunday afternoons were when my father, bearing the slumped shoulders of the condemned, came to see me. His visits took the form of drives. We always went to the closest possible fast food joint—an A&W drive-in about a mile from the house. I'd have a root beer float in a frosted mug while he waited, fingers a-drumming. The Bee Gees were usually playing, but this wouldn't be why his fingers were drumming. 'OK? You finished?' These were half-hour trips, tops.

One Sunday when I was eight, he took me to his (I thought, scary) walk-up rental and said I would be given dinner. It was five o'clock. Before he went and disappeared into the bathroom, he told me that if I got bored, I could always play a game of Monopoly or whatever. 'Just don't …'

I decided I would. And did. I tiptoed down the short hallway and delicately, accidentally peered through a partly opened door: unmade double bed, and above it, painted on the wall, Wendy the Good Little Witch riding her broom.

I had barely begun to absorb this when a woman with a big smile bounded out of the kitchen. She wore short shorts, exposing pale thunder thighs without a care, and oversized plastic glasses that made her ageless, at once chickadee and Mother Superior. The hair was sweat-flattened Doug Henning, but still fluffy above the brows. Before she could even say hi, she sneezed into her sleeve. I liked her immediately.

Her name was Doris. She loved comic books. And she was going to be my stepmother—once they got around to, you know, the paperwork. For now, if I could just hang on for a few minutes, she was cooking us dinner. This fact alone got my attention. I'd never known anyone, other than servants, who so much as boiled water. And the smells coming from the kitchen were at least four triple-axels up from the anodyne aromas of soy sauce braises and garlic stir-fries I associated with dinnertime at home. Chili pepper was at play here, sneeze-inducing amounts of it. What Doris served me that evening would change the way I saw the world, beginning with adults.

⇥

At twenty-one, Doris was already the veteran of a trio of Filipino action movies in which she starred as Interpol agent Cleopatra Wong. That was a lifetime ago, when she was eighteen and slender, and living in Manila with the director-impresario Bobby Suarez, whose cost-saving measures had Doris doing her own stunts, the most memorable of which was dangling from the base of a helicopter the day after her appendectomy. For the film *They Call Her Cleopatra Wong*, she was made to shoot arrows from a dirt bike and fire a four-barrel shotgun in a nun's habit. But the single most strenuous thing Suarez ever made her do was stay on a diet.

My father didn't care about any of that. The first time he saw her, she was shimmying in feathers and sequins, belly hanging out, lead dancer in a troupe called the Devil's Angels that performed weeknights at the Golden Million nightclub. He was a salesman, or between jobs, or something, fast approaching his mid-thirties. She was taller and rounder than him, but they liked to smoke, they laughed at the same dumb things, so it happened fast.

I grasped that it was now down to me, the kid, the last gauntlet their love had to brazen through, not because my approval mattered but because my existence affected how they carved up their Sundays. It was easiest if we could at least agree on food.

But harmony had to be improvised. Because they didn't have a dining table, my father prepared the coffee table, stabilizing its uneven feet with old copies of *Penthouse* and military magazines. A cushion with funny smells would have to make do as my seat. And since he didn't want to have to move the fish tank or the hi-fi so he and Doris could join me on the floor, they'd sit on the couch across from me, resting their plates on their thighs.

When Doris emerged, with a showbiz *ta-dah!* after hours of toil and panic in the kitchen, cleaning, cutting and reassembling from memory a flavor she thought she kind of knew but didn't quite really, the dish she produced was the notoriously labor-intensive sambal squid. Only later would I learn that this was the first time she'd ever cooked anything in her entire life, making it an even giddier leap of faith.

Under the buzzing bare-tube fluorescent light, I loved what I saw—food in Technicolor, food unlike that served at home. I'd had squid before, and timid pecks of chili, but not the two conjoined with such *joie de vivre*. Purple-pink squid tentacles and rings awash in a bright red chili sauce, the dense parts of the paste clinging to every crevice between the curlicue legs. The dish smelled—what, Malaysian? Indian? No, no, this was Indonesian—with garlic, shrimp paste, candlenuts and palm sugar in its DNA, not that I could classify it at the time as anything other than 'yummy', or a tad more rigorously as 'not home'. There were no side dishes; the rice was mushy, clearly budget-grain and cooked with a drunkard's care. Yet these details and the squid's actual taste (rubbery, under-salted) were immaterial. What struck me was that this child-woman I barely knew had cooked me something cool and different—and seemed mighty tickled at herself for having done it. Chili-burned, I scarfed down her joy, her unbridled exuberance, and asked for more.

I didn't pause to let my father and Doris have their share—they had wheels, they could always go out for Shakey's pizza later. I wanted to demonstrate to Doris my appreciation, my instant infatuation; I wanted to understand the state of mind that would let someone cook something this imperfect and feel *great* about it. Furthermore, though only as an afterthought, I really dug those new flavors, whatever they were!

After dinner, Doris and I sat on their bed—that unmade bed—and played Boggle while my father collapsed beside us and closed his eyes and farted. I lost because I spent most of the game marveling at the giant Wendy the Good Little Witch above the (headboard-less) top of the bed. I saw the faint pencil marks peeking out from under Wendy's red robe: somebody had drawn her outline and then painted her in—a vandal, twice over! At home, I wasn't even allowed to stick a Post-It on any surface in case the paint chipped. And then there was the bed—the unmarried bed—crumpled sheets, pillowcases that didn't match, and oh, the clammy smells.

'Do you like my Wendy?' Doris asked.

'Of course.'

'Do you like comics?'

'Of course.' In truth I'd had no experience with them apart from those glimpsed at newsstands. I had no idea who Wendy the Witch was aside from being Casper the Friendly Ghost's part-time chum. I read what I was supposed to—books about English boarding schools and goblins.

'Well, Doris here really, really loves comics.' My father, eyes still shut, gestured to the side of the bed where five stacks of well-thumbed comic books hugged the wall, rising from the floor like tombstones. 'She's got a thousand of them.' He wasn't exaggerating. He didn't sound thrilled.

I skimmed the ones near the top—all Archies. Grown-ups in '50s outfits playing at high school and bonking one another over the head. Fascinating.

'OK? You finished?' My father hadn't anticipated dinner to be such a smash. He'd been ready to take me home the minute I stepped in. Whatever had made their bed so messy—he wanted to get right back to it.

That night, when I told my grandmother and aunt what I'd been fed, they were flabbergasted, traditionalists that they were. What kind of a woman would *choose* to cook something like that? What kind of a dish is that to serve a guest, least of all a child? This reaction I found delightful, though glee behaved as it often did in that household and quickly disintegrated into self-doubt. Was I wrong to like it? Was I disloyal to like *her*?

Sambal squid became a guilty pleasure. It meant dinner away from home, away from the staid and the disapproving. It

made me happy to eat it, and it seemed to make Doris happy
to cook it. I didn't want anything to change. So why not keep it
simple? I requested it Sunday after Sunday, so much so that my
father thought I was secretly mocking him (and he knew I had
the propensity for this, having been raised by snobs and nags
and hypocrites). Sometimes the dish was good and sometimes
it was mediocre, but I always ate it with gusto, savoring the
ritual of dining with two grown-ups who shared the same
stinky, witch-anointed bed. So this was what it felt like to be in
a nuclear family. So this was what my classmates, my cousins,
even the stupidest people in the world had. Sunday dinner with
my own family ... Come on, let's do this thing forever.

made me happy to eat it, and it seemed to make Doris happy

Then, because romances do this, things hit a bump. My
father brought a black crow to Chinese New Year lunch at my
grandmother's, the annual gathering of relatives thankful
there was only one such annual gathering. All the cousins
and uncles and aunts—lukewarm Dr. Scholl's types—smiled
politely then whispered about the strange lady in the black
dress, black fishnet stockings, high heels, eyeliner, mascara,
nails, black nearly everything. I watched the woman from
across the room, and she watched me back. It was Doris,
of course, but Doris dolled up in a form I'd never known.
Such sad, cruel eyes the makeup gave her. She didn't smile,
barely shook hands, hardly said a word. Where were her
goofy glasses? Her underarm sweat-rings? I'd never even seen
her wear lip gloss and here she was with deep-red mistress
mouth, sitting with a cup of tea she wouldn't touch. The

aunts who'd seen her before now revised their old verdict of 'bubbly'. My grandmother didn't need to say a word for me to know what she was thinking. She had only to smile: instead of having shark's fin and roast goose with us, you *chose* to eat food prepared by this witch?

I ran and hid until everybody left.

In the months that followed, I still saw my father and Doris on Sundays, though less often for dinner—mainly just nowhere drives. It was a tight fit for the three of us in the MG, with me having to jackknife myself behind the two bucket seats. It made my father laugh to see me squashed against the burning vinyl of the soft top, and he'd speed up to 90 mph so he could cackle some more. 'Poor Boo-Boo!' he'd say, for some reason having decided I was the spoilsport tagalong bear in the Yogi cartoons.

Sometime in that period, they actually got married. She'd been right. There was no ceremony; it was just paperwork, after all. Then Chinese New Year arrived again. Neither my father nor Doris attended the annual lunch, but hours later, while I was watching a Tom Jones special on TV, Doris showed up shaking and in tears. Blue jeans this time, and no makeup. Like the New Year prior, the two of us looked at each other but made no actual contact. She ran straight to my grandmother and blurted: my father chased her around with a meat cleaver, gangs were involved, she'd slept the previous nights with scissors under her pillow, and the police—she had called the police. My grandmother hushed her and took her to another room. Half an hour later, Doris left. The cops didn't drop by, or perhaps they did and my grandmother sent them away so smoothly in her genteel way that it registered as a non-event even to me.

Doris never returned, yet the rupture was so swiftly disowned in our house that whenever her name was brought up, she was always referred to as 'that nice girl'. My father eventually resurfaced many Sundays later, his car laden with Archie comics. He asked if I'd take them off his hands. If so, it'd be two more trips for him to complete the transfer. I said yes, then asked the crucial questions: But what if she wanted them back? And what about Wendy the Witch—did he paint over her? My father sighed. 'OK? You finished?'

He turned his car around and stepped on the gas.

JAY RAYNER is a writer, journalist, and broadcaster. He is the restaurant critic for the *London Observer*, has a fine collection of flowery shirts, and likes pig. His latest book is *A Greedy Man in a Hungry World: How (Almost) Everything You Thought You Knew About Food Is Wrong*.

THE OYSTER MEN

Jay Rayner

The first time I got it wrong. The first time, I was forced to lose most of an afternoon to the very waters that had gifted me my lunch. Then again, the ways of the sea have never exactly been my strong point. It's a cultural marker, this lack of ocean smarts. It's the non-Jews who have the boats. It's the non-Jews who understand the way that wind and canvas can be made to dance with each other so as to speed the journey out across the surface. My lot prefer to stay on dry land. When Moses needed to get his tribe across the Red Sea he didn't summon a flotilla. He got a friend to draw back the waters to the harder, firmer stuff beneath. I am a Jew. It makes sense that I should not think about the way the tides would impact upon my eating and travel plans.

This, of course, is ludicrous special pleading. For while I eagerly push my Jewishness into service as an excuse for getting caught out on Mersea Island, off the coast of Essex, I discard it with just as much enthusiasm, so I can eat the essence of non-kosher seafood which is its speciality: the glistening, pearly oysters that have been nurtured in these parts since Roman times. The Jewish God is far too picky an eater for me to have any time for him. The facts are these. I didn't do my research. I understood that I could reach the seafood cafe I wanted to visit via a cab ride from Colchester Station, forty-five minutes' train ride to the north-east of London. It didn't for a moment occur to me that this access might not be permanent; that the high tides could sweep in across the Strood, the causeway that links the island to the mainland, making it impassable, and leave me stranded for a few hours. As I sat at the table that first time, necking my oysters and picking at my crab, that's exactly what happened. I had to wait a few hours for the waters to recede before the cab could rescue me. There are worse places to be.

I am an old hand now. I am experienced. When the hankering for great seafood comes over me, I begin by looking at the tide tables to find out exactly when the high waters will cover the causeway that links this most easterly of inhabited islands in the United Kingdom to the rest of England. It is worth the effort. The fractured landscape of the Essex coast, where earth and sea seem to crumble into each other, is one of Britain's great larders. It is not just the oysters—both the flat, round natives, and their less aristocratic cousins, the comma-shaped rocks—but also the snowy soft crystals of salt produced by boiling up the sea at Maldon on the Blackwater River.

I decide I need a companion. I call up my friend David, a musician who once played mandolin and saw in the Irish punk folk band the Pogues, but who admits he was always more interested in the food on tour than the *craic*. Now he's respectable. Now he works as a musical director for the likes of Tom Waits, Marianne Faithful and the Tiger Lillies. He still treats touring as an eating opportunity, and he will travel for lunch. In hushed tones I explain to him the premise and the premises: a place called the Company Shed, which really is little more than a shed, but where they serve some of the best seafood you are ever likely to eat in Britain. They provide the shellfish, the cutlery and the crockery. We will have to bring the rest.

We meet at Liverpool Street Station, in the City of London. Solemnly David shows me the bottle of Muscadet Sèvre et Maine he has bought for the occasion, which he says is the only white wine to drink with oysters. He has a couple of bottles of ink-dark Porter ale plus a bottle of soy sauce and a tube of wasabi paste. David's wife is Japanese-American and he has learnt from her that you do not approach seafood without these things. I have a jar of Hellmann's mayonnaise. There is no point making your own mayonnaise when Hellmann's can make it so much better. We are equipped.

It is a cliché that journeys in search of great food must have a certain rugged glamour and bravado to them: there are the suicidal hairpin bends of the Italian mountains, which must be navigated to find salamis made the way Italian grandmas have always made them; there are the drives beneath huge Texan skies in search of the best barbecue. The journey to the

Company Shed has no glamour. It's pig ugly. It's a journey through other people's narrow horizons and despair. The train ride takes you out past the mournful industrial remains of the Olympic Park, now being dismantled, and then down through the endless grey suburbia of north-east London and Essex. Occasionally you sight fields, but they quickly give way to the back view of dull domestic English life: scabbed gardens with sagging washing lines, netted trampolines for the kids and bored dogs left to bark at the passing carriages while their owners are out at work. It would all smell of damp and soot, had not the careless thrill of domestic fires been banned so long ago.

Colchester, once the Roman capital of Britain, has a great heritage. Not that you'd know it from the bleak, modern train station, or from the cab that drives us away from it. The car smells lightly of damp dog. The rear seat is covered by a tartan rug; air fresheners hang from the mirror. Blunt, low-slung modern houses edge the highways out of town apologetically, separated only by the occasional scrubby fields. Eventually we break out of half-hearted woodland to dash across the Strood, like kids making for homey in a game of tag. On a dull, late winter's day at low tide the waters that lap at either side of the causeway are the colour of used engine oil. The journey across the causeway is over as soon as it has begun and we are finally on the island of Mersea, though still it stubbornly refuses to be pretty. There are a few switchbacks, past unassuming, dead-eyed pubs, and newsagents and semi-detached houses chosen by their owners as retirement boltholes.

Until finally we are on the coast road and the first moment of a bleak kind of beauty: salt marshes and reed banks spread out towards the waters, punctuated by wooden houseboats perched high on blocks. The tides here can rise and fall by as much as six metres so the boats need to be lifted off the ground. We snake past boatsheds, and crammed boat yards, full of yachts with their masts tilted to the bruising gull-infested sky.

At last we are there. The Company Shed is a simple, single-storey, black-painted slat-board building. It looks like nothing. It looks like the annexe for something else that is also nothing. In the summer, queues an hour or more long build up outside it. The cafe was opened more than a quarter of a century ago by Heather Haward, wife of a legendary oysterman in these parts called Richard Haward. He can trace his family's involvement in the oyster business back seven generations. There are records from 1792 of his ancestor William Haward taking oysters up the Thames to the fish market at Billingsgate, and this Haward still gets oysters to the capital on a daily basis.

Heather wanted a job for weekends, to give her something to do while raising the children, so she launched the shop and cafe. These days it's open six days a week, but the notion hasn't changed much. At busy times you chalk your name on a blackboard and wait to be called to one of the oil-skin-covered tables, most of them communal. Regulars, the sort of elders of the tribe who are able to slack off on a weekday lunchtime, arrive with cool bags full of wine and baguettes. They know how it works. They know what they are doing.

At the front is a slab with wet fish to buy, and a counter with a few smoked products. At the back is a tiny kitchen from which come a couple of cooked dishes a day.

We order those: fat seared scallops on a tomato and bacon salad, and some king prawns, roasted in their shells, with a spicy mayonnaise. They start us up, like jump leads to a frozen car engine. What really matters, though, is the oysters. We order a dozen of the natives: the ones that come from the waters at our backs and which were filtered in the sheds just through the door over my shoulder. There are half a dozen of the prime number ones and half a dozen of the slightly smaller number twos and they cost around half of what they would in the sort of London restaurants which make such a big thing about supplying bread, and having a wine list and carpets.

Both sets are bright and fresh and meaty. Eating them is like being slapped around the face with spray off the bow of a wave-crashing yawl. We try them with a splash of Tabasco, one of the few condiments they do offer, and a dribble of the soy, punched up with wasabi. Quickly they disappear. We get the seafood platter, with its folds of locally smoked salmon and mackerel, the latter soothed by my jar of mayo. There are tiny prawns, and bigger shrimps and a pouch of smoked cod's roe with that taste neatly balanced between sweet and smoke and bitter. Out the back door we can see clouds of steam rising. I stand up to get a better view. Dozens of crabs the size of dinner plates have just come out of the boiler. The crabs are not from around here, but they bring them in alive and keep them in filtration tanks in the cafe alongside the lobsters. Then they boil them as needed.

One of them is on our plate, and we sit contentedly, picking the white meat out of the more knotty and complicated bits of the shell, piling up the strands and then dressing them with soy and wasabi. It doesn't feel like an overly cosmopolitan thing to do. The Company Shed, though bare and rough about the edges, is a place where nations meet. By the door is a party of young Japanese people, who have come to do silent damage to lobsters, the shells heaped in the middle of the table, the debris of a special sort of gustatory war. Behind us is an Australian couple, who declare it the best seafood they have ever eaten. 'Outside Oz, of course.' Well, of course. The rest of our table is taken up by a trio of expat Greek men who live nearby in Chelmsford. There, they run Greek restaurants. When they have a little free time they come here to do things to crabs. They share the fresh bread they baked this morning. We give them glasses of our Porter. It's that sort of place.

Slowly we admit defeat. We would like to eat more. We would like the journey to continue. But shellfish like this always starts out bright and fresh before becoming first rich, then enough and finally too much. Richard Haward appears by our table. He's a big grizzly heap of a man, with a straggly white beard and teeth like an overgrown graveyard. Early one morning, a year or two back, he took me out in an oyster boat, in a cold relentless rain, and stood in the prow looking like a part of the ancient landscape. I remember him cutting his thumb badly while shucking an oyster straight off one of the beds. I remember the way he didn't flinch or even seem to notice. He bled into the sea, giving a part of himself to the waters as the Hawards always have. Now he stood quietly beside us. How was it, he wanted to know. I shrugged at the wreckage on the table in front of us. It was as it always is here, I told him, a special kind of perfect. He nodded solemnly and moved away.

After lunch we went for a short walk along the coast road while we waited for our cab to collect us and I told David about my first time there: about how, during my lunch, someone I was sharing the table with had watched me packing my things away at the end of my meal. My fellow diner had glanced at his watch and told me I wouldn't be going anywhere. 'Mersea's an island again,' he had said. 'Don't worry. It's only for a few hours.' I saw the look on David's face. I knew what he was thinking. He liked the sound of that. He liked the idea of being marooned here, so close to such perfect seafood, even if only temporarily. It wouldn't be happening today, though. The high tide wasn't until much later in the afternoon. This time I had done my homework. I nodded down the road. Our cab was approaching. It was time to go home.

Since coining the term Roadfood and pointing the way to America's best eats, **JANE AND MICHAEL STERN** have written more than 40 books about American food and popular culture. Their website, Roadfood.com, pioneered internet food reporting and photography. They regularly contribute to *Saveur* and *Parade* magazines.

SOUTHERN EXPOSURE

Jane and Michael Stern

The short-order cook standing at the griddle at the Adam and Eve Diner looked back over his shoulder and asked us, 'How do you want dem eggs?' He was a burly guy, well over six feet tall, wearing a puffy chef's toque, a white t-shirt, and an apron tied at the waist. As he faced away from us to crack our eggs and shuffle hash browns on the griddle, our seats on stools at the counter afforded us a direct view of his pink bare buttocks. Regulars at the Adam and Eve knew him as Southern Exposure.

We don't spend much time dining at strip clubs, so it was a little strange to eat a meal surrounded by naked and semi-naked cooks, waitresses and customers. But that's the way it was when we stopped in the Adam and Eve Diner in 1974. The Adam and Eve was part of the Naked City Truck Stop in Roselawn, Indiana, about an hour south of Gary.

There is not much to do in Roselawn. It is in a particularly drab part of America—a web of flat roads, fast food joints, plain architecture, and mobile homes. There is nothing of the rolling Grant Wood Midwest here, or the dramatic wheat-filled blankness of Nebraska. It is not nostalgic or romantic; it is simply bare and sad.

If you lived in Roselawn you might understand the urge to do something radical to break the boredom. You might say one day, as you are having toast and coffee, 'Hey, I have a great idea. Let's open a truck stop where the waitresses and cook are naked and customers are free to strip if they'd like.' If you lived in the midst of pounding boredom it might seem like a plan.

In 1968, a man named Dick Drost had this light-bulb-over-the-head moment. He opened a truck stop and called it Naked City. As strange as Drost's idea was, Roselawn, Indiana, already had seen more than its share of naked people. It was in this tiny town on the Jasper and Newton County line that a Chicago lawyer named Alois Knapp opened Club Zoro in 1933—billed as the largest nudist colony in America. Knapp, who originally came from Austria, was the founder and editor of *Sunshine and Health* magazine, the archetypal nature culture digest that shows nudists to be healthy, happy folks playing volleyball and bridge despite the fact that they have no genitals (thanks to early airbrushing techniques).

Dale and Mary Drost (Dick's father and mother) bought the nudist colony from Knapp in the 1940s and ran it until their son took over and named it Naked City. Dick had big plans for the acreage east of I-65 on Route 10. Because of its proximity to a major highway, where Peterbilts and Kenworths thundered by day and night, he saw the creaky old nudist colony as a potential tourist attraction, where truckers and civilians would come to eat hearty portions of gearjammer grub served by sexy naked waitresses. His plans were grand. He envisioned strip shows and topless beauty contests, visitors relaxing in communal hot tubs and spending the night in rustic bunkhouses surrounded by chirping naked nature.

There were a few problems in the master plan right from the beginning.

Most nudist colonies are in sunny climates and cater to naturists of the 'nuts and berries' type: clean-living sun-worshipers, tanned and vigorous. Roselawn, Indiana, is cold and grey for half the year and humid and buggy the other half. This part of the Midwest is not known for its health consciousness. In fact, the typical restaurant meal consists of deep-fried pork tenderloin the size of a dinner plate on a squishy supermarket bun and a dish of soft-serve custard ice cream for dessert.

As Naked City's figurehead, Dick Drost was not the picture of health. Crippled and twisted by muscular dystrophy, he whizzed around Naked City in a motorized wheelchair with a raccoon tail dangling off the back. He wanted to be the next Hugh Hefner, but he was twisted both mentally and physically, and did not have the funds to support his grandiose ideas. The best he could do was buy a round bed and cover it with a tatty sequined cover and have friends take pictures of him surrounded by a bevy of naked white-trash beauties.

When we visited Naked City a few years after it opened, the place already looked worn and fetid. The hot tub bubbled with blue green algae, the sexy naked women looked decidedly unfresh, and there was a disturbing number of underage girls milling around, waiting for the Miss Naked Teenybopper contest to begin. The truckers, most of whom kept their clothes on, seemed immune to the seediness, happy to eat some grub and see bare tits. Naked City became their playground; there was always something to celebrate at the end of the long haul. They showed up in force for holiday events like the Saint Patrick's Day celebration called Erin Go-Braless. They strolled around the park and enjoyed Drost's grand monument: a 63-foot-long sculpture of a shapely lady's leg wearing a black high heel. The leg was decidedly Art Brut, but with a purpose. It functioned as a sundial—a clever inspiration for nudists who shed their watches along with their clothing.

Drost's original vision of Naked City was as broad as Walt Disney's for Disneyland, even imagining franchised Naked Cities all over the world. Ultimately, he saw literal naked cities, 'with buildings, skyscrapers, and people doing everything and anything that they would in a medium-size city … in the nude'. The fount of it all would be the truck stop and its Adam and Eve Diner—a sure moneymaker because truck drivers who worked the network of highways that passed along Roselawn needed to eat. The menu attracted drivers for its featured 'gearjammer breakfast' of three eggs, three biscuits, hash browns, chicken-fried steak drowned in a pool of thick white cream gravy, along with unlimited cups of insipid pale brown coffee.

At that point of our career we were interested in the culture of long-haul truck drivers. We believed them to be the last American cowboys and we made it our work to see life as they did. As we sat at the counter in the Adam and Eve, waiting for our home fries and eggs, we were greeted by Miss Nude America, Cheryl Turner, who served as hostess. Except for high-heel shoes, Cheryl was completely naked, although she did carry around a small patch of shag rug to put on chairs so her ass wouldn't stick to the Lucite or Naugahyde. Bleached blonde with gravity-resistant breast implants, she walked from customer to customer offering little plastic combs imprinted with the words Naked City Truck Stop. For a few dollars, truckers were invited to comb her tuft of pubic hair and keep the comb as a souvenir. For a few dollars more, you could buy a Reddi-Wip and honey dessert, with Miss Nude America serving as the human plate. Whether it was the strain of hours on the road or just the bizarre, unreal quality of life in a nude truck stop, there was a strange lack of sexual tension in the air.

Inspired by Southern Exposure's blush-colored behind, we supplemented our potatoes and eggs with two portions of thick-sliced country ham. Say what you will about the rest of Naked City, it was damn good ham: sizzled crisp on the griddle and served with red-eye gravy and canned biscuits hot from the oven. We actually kind of liked the place. It certainly was one of a kind. The jukebox blasted fine old

Hank Williams tunes and newer Jerry Reed ones, and we even bought one of Miss Nude America's souvenir combs, but decided against the grooming option.

Naked City did not age well. Dick Drost's dream of opening a chain of Naked City Truck Stops all around the country, and eventually the world, never came to be; and old-style, physical-fitness naturists in the tradition of Alois Knapp learned to shun the shenanigans for which the nudist resort became notorious. After a few run-ins with the law, Drost closed Naked City in 1986, pleading guilty to ten sex-related misdemeanors and agreeing to stay out of Indiana for ten years.

After years of neglect, Naked City was reborn as Sun Aura Resort, where the lady leg sundial remains, clothing is optional, and organized fun is pretty much limited to weekend dances by the bonfire. One mile east, the Ponderosa Sun Club carries on the Dick Drost spirit of naked revelry. Despite its proclaimed family-friendly principles ('a public erection is not acceptable'), it hosts a yearly Nudes-A-Poppin Festival in July, with competitions for Miss & Mr. Nude Go-Go, Miss & Mr. Nude North America, Miss Nude Erotic Pole Performer, and an amateur wet t-shirt contest.

As far as we can tell, there are no more good ham steaks to eat in Roselawn, Indiana. Southern Exposure long ago hung up his toque, put on his pants, and moved on to sunnier climes.

M.J. HYLAND is the author of three multi-award-winning novels: *How the Light Gets In, Carry Me Down,* and *This Is How.* Hyland also lectures in creative writing and is co-founder of The Hyland & Byrne Editing Firm.

HOW TO EAT
FOR FREE
IN HELSINKI

M.J. Hyland

In Melbourne's business district, one very hot day in January 2001, I walked into a budget travel agency and booked a flight to Helsinki.

I had no special interest in Helsinki, and the cost of the ticket left me broke, but I couldn't stomach the swelter of summer and I wanted to spend some time in a colder place, a city in the dark of winter.

On that day I'd no idea of the trouble coming: that in seven years I'd be diagnosed with multiple sclerosis. And I didn't know that I'd also suffer from a disease within a disease— Uhthoff's syndrome—a set of MS symptoms which cause profound heat intolerance.

I wasn't sick in January 2001, not one bit sick, and I had just two problems: Melbourne's hot weather and the deep boredom of working as a corporate lawyer on the 88th floor of a city law firm.

An hour before booking the flight, I was in Collins Street with a senior associate, a man with a big ego and female hips who loved both the sun and the law.

'Jesus,' he said, 'I'd give anything to be down the beach.'

'Yeah,' I said. 'That'd be nice.'

It wouldn't be nice. The last time I went to the beach I was shitty and sore and kept all my clothes on—a long-sleeved shirt, socks and shoes—and my head was covered with a wet towel.

'Can we cross the street?' I said. 'And walk in the shade?'

We were on our way to the Supreme Court to hear the verdict of an industrial-relations dispute.

'Why?' he said. 'It's only three blocks.'

He looked at me as though he wanted to spit on my head, and no surprise. I hated the sun, which he loved, I was a useless and indifferent lawyer and, unlike him, I didn't bill enough hours or make budget.

The associate, on the other hand, made money and, like most corporate lawyers, he'd started law school with good intentions, and now his conscience was stashed away in the receipts drawer of Tiffany & Co.

'So, could we?' I said, 'Cross the road?'

'What?'

'Walk on the other side of the street?' I said. 'There's some shade over there.'

'Why?'

'Don't worry,' I said. 'Forget about it.'

We'd finished in the Supreme Court and on the way back to the office I told him I needed to run a quick errand.

'Don't forget the LXXX has to be filed by close of play today,' he said.

Close of play.

'Yes, yes,' I said, 'I just need to pop into the chemist.'

'Are you on all fours with the PXXX file?' he asked.

On all fours—that's lawyer-talk and it proves you need a high I.Q. Most lawyers don't say anything real, and most of them are afraid of small words.

When you're a lawyer, you should sound expert all day long and this means using platitudes, and every one, every time, must be spoken as though it's an original term of art, reserved for a special world.

Lawyers don't say: How are you getting on with the PXX file? They say: Are you across the PXX file? Or, Are you up to speed? And worse, Are you on all fours?

'Oh, yes,' I said. 'I'll have all that done by tonight.'

'And the due diligence for TXXX?'

'Yes, I'm across that too,' I said.

I smiled. I was glad we'd lost our case.

'It looks like our client was an unconscionable maggot-hole,' I said. 'And he was obviously guilty of diabolical acts of Rachmanism.'

—————

I had a lawyer for a boyfriend once, and he turned up at my flat late on a Friday night, huffing and puffing. He said he had something urgent to discuss, and then he proposed:

'Marcus thinks you're a real catch,' he said. 'And he's probably right.'

Marcus was a lawyer too.

'That's nice,' I said.

'So, what would you say,' he said, 'in the event that I asked you to marry me?'

⇥

Outside the office on Collins Street, the senior associate told me to come see him for 'a head's up' when I'd finished with my errand. Ten minutes later, I was in the travel agency spending money I couldn't afford to lose on an ASAP flight to Helsinki and all because, in the agency's window, I saw pictures of Helsinki wearing its snowy white coat:

'… In late January the mercury can fall to below -15°C … and the sea freezes over.'

The travel agent told me about a new hotel near the central train station.

'It's absolutely wonderful,' she said.

'It's so cheap,' I said.

'Probably because it's new,' she said.

I asked her to book ten nights.

'Won't you be wanting to stop anywhere else?'

'No, thanks.'

'It's winter in Helsinki,' she said.

'I know,' I said. 'I like the cold. My favourite people are Shackleton, Scott and Mawson and they'll be in my first novel.'

⇥

During the twenty-six-hour flight with Qantas, I made plans. I'd book a train to Northern Finland to see the aurora borealis, hire a snow sled with four black-eyed huskies who'd mush me through blizzards. I could call 'gee' and 'haw' with a blanket on my lap and, if the conditions were extreme, 'duct tape for the face' which, according to the travel guides, should prevent frostbite.

Scandinavian food involves lots of fish so I asked the man in 14C to teach me how to say 'I think there's something fishy going on here in Finland' but as he rightly pointed out, this pun wouldn't work in translation.

'How about: I'd like to watch the fishermen fishing for fishes in Finnish ice-holes?' I said.

The man in 14C had a few more drinks.

At Helsinki-Vantaa's taxi rank, the air was so cold it made my skin sting and when I unzipped my suitcase, my fingers were numb and sore—as though bruised. But I was more alive, wide awake, no lucid indifference now. I was sharper in the snow and already happier. I was still happy when I got to the hotel and saw that Huone 18 was cheap because it was smaller than a holding cell under a cop-house.

For three days I went for walks through the city, brisk in my Doc Marten boots on streets of ice and snow. I sat in a café with a view of the Baltic Sea and watched ferries and ice-breakers crunching a path to Estonia and St Petersburg.

In the late afternoon, when it got too cold for walking, I went to Strindberg Café and read Ibsen, Strinberg and the grotty Timo K. Mukka. On the fourth day, I bought a ticket for a Sibelius concert in Finlandia Hall, withdrew a lump of spending money, and checked my bank balance.

I was broke.

I'd been an idiot. I was a lawyer and earned good money but I had debts, and I'd run out of favours. I wasn't only bust, but trapped in Helsinki for a week with no more than the equivalent of $18 a day or 76 Finnish markka.

I've always preferred the cold and the dark of winter, but I didn't want to be cold in Helsinki, not if I couldn't spend money on nice hot food and excursions up north or husky rides or a trip to watch the ice-fishing.

Like most people, I've got more than one fear. In 2001, as well as my dread of summer, I had an equal dread of being poor, of living a straightened and botched life; a fear of not being able to get my hands on luxury or extravagance—a fear of ending up bust and broken like my mum and dad and brother.

⇢⊪⟋

In the intermission at the Sibelius concert, I sat in the foyer and watched people who had plenty of both food and money and they were eating a feast of cakes and pastries and drinking strong, hot coffee.

I was hungry and wanted cake and coffee.

I went to the bar. Maybe I could afford a small slice of *kinuski-kermakakku* (a caramel cream cake).

'How much for just one slice and a small cup of coffee?' I asked.

'There is no further cake left,' said the barman. 'It was necessary to pre-book.'

He was with regret.

'Will you order a drink?'

'No, thanks. I want cake.'

Just like Tolstoy's white bear, triple-layer chocolate cream cake, once mentioned, can't be ignored or forgotten and, from my armchair in the corner of the foyer I sulked and stewed in my hunger.

Then I had an idea. I'd do something I hadn't done since university: the 'pass-over'. I'd lift some leftover cake and biscuits (*keksi*) from an abandoned table.

Although there was plenty of time left before the concert started—at least fifteen minutes, maybe more—a young couple got up from their table and headed back to the auditorium. There are always people who return to their seats early. They are fretful and conservative types, the same kind of people who won't sit in a train carriage unless it's the exact seat they've been allocated, and they won't move even if there's a more comfortable seat across the aisle or in the next carriage. Without them, 'the pass-over' wouldn't be possible.

I took a book from my bag and dropped it near the abandoned table and, as I bent down to pick up the book, I made sure my backpack swiped at a cup of coffee, causing spillage. Next, I pretended to clean up and used a napkin to scoop a slice of leftover cake and some biscuits, too.

This manoeuvre is surprisingly easy. By the time waiters realise what's happened, and they come to the table all worry and wiping, I've stashed what I want, and nobody's the wiser.

Back in my armchair in Finlandia Hall's grand foyer, I ate the cake and got more proof that food tastes better in cold climates. No cake had ever tasted as good as this cake tasted.

In hot weather, I get hungry, of course, but only at the top of my stomach. And the day of the concert, I'd been outside all afternoon in the freezing frost and my hunger was deeper and the eating was better.

The concert ended late, nearly midnight, and it was too cold for walking. My saliva might freeze and I had no earmuffs, or duct tape, and so I caught a taxi to the hotel and used half of next day's money.

Being broke was a nuisance, but not an emergency: Helsinki's a beautiful, compact city, and there's plenty to see for free. But having no money meant not eating in restaurants, and this bothered me most of all. There was a supermarket near the hotel, and I'd have plenty of bread and jam, but it pissed me off that I'd come all this way to eat bananas and biscuits.

I decided I'd eat on the cheap during the day, and at night, go to a fancy restaurant near Market Square and order the soup, or whatever was the cheapest thing on the menu. Eating even a small portion in a flash restaurant was a whole lot better than nothing at all. And my it mattered to me, perhaps too much, that I'd escaped a life of poverty and grunge for a life of privilege and if I couldn't eat my dinner in flash restaurants—after all my efforts and study, scholarships and prizes—I might as well call myself a failure, like the rest of my family.

The next day, I stayed in my room and learnt some Finnish:

'I'm very sorry, but I'd like to have the soup, but nothing else' and 'I feel sad'.

When somebody said, 'Why are you sad?' I'd say, 'I've lost my mittens.'

I also learnt to say, 'I'd like to sample more dishes on this lovely menu, but I don't have much time.'

And I learnt how to say, 'I'm a lawyer, but not a crooked one' and 'Finnish food is far superior to Swedish food.'

If somebody said, 'Really?' or 'Why?' I'd say, 'Swedish food tastes like a poet's raincoat.'

———※———

The first fancy restaurant I tried was right across from Market Square and had a beautiful, snowy view. It was early, half-past six, and I sat at the unfortunate table: every restaurant has an unfortunate table, and this one was close to the toilets.

There were four other diners, two couples. The men wore flashy suits and the women had crispy, sprayed, wig-like hair. They were rich and they smelt rich, and the women were so thin that even inside their big coats they had no bulk.

The waiter wasn't busy, but he didn't bother coming to my toilet-side table. He looked at me when I first came in, but after that, he paid me no mind.

While I waited, I looked round, a hard and long examination. Doing this hard-looking is more than a cure for boredom; it's the only proper way to live, though some of my friends don't agree: 'You're like a cop behind a two-way mirror' and, 'You're like an alien. It's like you've never seen anything before'.

By the time the waiter came, I was very hungry and wanted everything on the menu: *avokukko* (open-faced fish loaf) and moose mousse, pike with mushrooms and wild-berry sauce, reindeer with lingonberry sauce and chanterelles, blue-mussel soup, slow-fried lavaret (whitefish), mushroom crepes and traditional desserts, such as strawberry milk and doughnuts with coffee pudding. But an entrée cost €14.50 and a main cost €28.00 and I'd have to stick to a bowl of pea and ham soup.

I made sure the waiter saw me writing with a Montblanc pen. I also made sure—by rolling up my sleeve—that he saw my watch, which was a gift from a rich lawyer who smelt like old vase-water. It was TW Steel with sapphire crystal, and worth a small fortune.

'I'm very sorry,' I said. 'I'd like to have the soup, but nothing else. Is that possible?'

'With our pleasure,' he said.

I did some writing then, made notes as though in secret, waited until the maître d' and waiter were in the kitchen, and when the waiter was near my table I put the notebook away, and quickly.

The soup came with a basket of bread rolls, each a different shade. I ate all six and slowly and went on looking round, went on making notes.

⋙⋙

The waiter asked if I was satisfied.

'Yes,' I said. '*Kitos*.'

He made a long speech, and I'd no idea what he said, but I nodded and smiled and asked for the bill. He made another speech, then came back with a plate of food.

I think I said: 'No, thank you. I am not hungry. I would just like some water please. And the bill.'

He smiled, and I saw his teeth.

'*Kitos paljon*,' I said. (Thank you very much.)

He said something else. I think I said: '*Kitos … että oli erittäin maukasta, mutta minun täytyy lähteä nyt*.' (Thank you. That was lovely, but I need to go now.)

⋙⋙

If there'd been a mistake, so be it. It wasn't my fault. So, I ate all the food. The waiter came back with yet another plate and the maître d' kept watch from his station, his back pressed against the bar.

The third serving was bigger than the last: six morsels of fish, fishes in pastry, fish with noodles, scallops, and fish thingies inside tempura and a sea-yoke floating in a bowl of tasty water.

I didn't waste any time worrying about being asked to pay. I was happy. I'd made my mind up: the waiter must've mistaken me for a food critic, or a reviewer, and why? I'll never know for sure. When I'd told him that I only wanted the soup, I suppose I tried to compensate, and assert myself, and I said I was a lawyer, and something like this:

'I would like more food, but I am a lawyer. I need to go to my hotel. I must make an important phone call.'

Maybe the waiter thought, who is this person? No lawyer in the world dresses the way she does. If she's not a lawyer, then what is she, this woman?

My baggy jumper was too shiny to be made of wool and my hair looked like a mistake (I'd cut it myself) and my torn Crumpler backpack was held together with an Occy-strap.

The bill came and I hadn't been charged a penny for the extra food. I paid only for the bowl of soup and no more. My mood soared all the more when the maître d' said, 'For your pleasure, madam.'

Tomorrow was going to be a great day. I'd walk during the bright hours and spend the darkness somewhere warm, maybe the patisserie that looked out at the Art Nouveau train station, or I'd have a hot chocolate in that place near the harbour and scout for food.

I'd definitely get some 'pass-over' in Strindberg Café—where most people, who had too much of things, didn't seem able to eat a whole piece of *Omenapiiras ja vaniljakastiketta* (apple pie with vanilla sauce), especially not after they'd eaten a plate full of *graavilohiruisleipä, kananmunaa ja mummonkurkkuja* (rye bread with lightly salted salmon, egg and pickled cucumbers).

So, I would. I'd finish for them.

CURTIS STONE is an Australian chef, television personality and *New York Times* bestselling author. He's the host of Bravo's culinary competition *Top Chef Masters* and appears regularly on shows including *The Today Show*, *Ellen*, *Conan*, *The Talk* and *The Chew*. His fifth cookbook, *What's for Dinner?: Recipes for a Busy Life*, was released in April 2013.

AN ITALIAN EDUCATION

Curtis Stone

Somewhere in a drawer back home in Australia, there's a photo of me standing in the Melbourne International Airport. I'm wearing a wide-brimmed outback hat and holding a beat-up Australian football under my arm. A gigantic backpack looms behind my head, dwarfing my 6-foot 3-inch frame. I'm twenty-one years old and feeling like I'm the first Aussie to ever set foot outside the Commonwealth.

It was 1998, the year Monica Lewinsky's stained blue dress almost impeached a president and the European Central Bank was born in Frankfurt, Germany. It was also the year that I first travelled outside of Australia, and I had that particular blend of swagger and stupidity that young men have when they get their first real taste of freedom.

In hindsight that photo is the beginning of adventures that are still unfolding today. But when I posed for it, I only knew what had ended—culinary school. After four years studying and working every conceivable station at the Savoy Hotel in Melbourne, I was officially a chef. In those days, all the best chefs were European, so I reckoned that after school I'd head to Europe to study with the masters. While I was filleting barramundi and julienning carrots, I saved like a man with a plan. When culinary school ended, I sold my sky-blue Datsun 200B and counted the till; I had ten thousand Australian dollars to my name, which meant I could travel for roughly three months on $100 a day. When the money was gone, I'd need to find a job.

That budget added up for my best mate Tommy, who was working for his dad as a concreter at the time. Tommy and I had been thick as thieves since high school. He was that kid who would lean against a wall at a party with his arms crossed and a sly smile lifting one side of his mouth, just taking it all in. He was the quintessential fly on the wall, which explains why everyone called him Tommy the Fly. Tommy was also mad about soccer, an obsession I never really understood, as Aussie Rules was my game, and that summer he was headed to the FIFA World Cup in Paris. So we hatched a plan to meet after the finals in Pamplona, Spain, for the running of the bulls.

Actually a plan might be stretching it. We looked at a map and agreed to meet at two o'clock on a day in July at the entrance to the Plaza del Castillo, the main square in Pamplona. We'd figure it out from there. So I boarded my first ever international flight, from Melbourne to Rome, sure of nothing more than I'd need to catch a train from the Italian capital to Spain.

Naïve trust is both the beauty and the downfall of being a young adult. It's the set of blinders that makes you braver than you realise and more foolish than you'll ever be again. It gets you on a flight to Europe without knowing a word of Italian or Spanish and helps you gesture your way onto all the right trains so that you're miraculously standing at the entrance of the Plaza del Castillo at two o'clock on the agreed day in July with a money belt strapped under your shirt.

Only Tommy wasn't there. What had looked like a charming little town green on the map turned out to be an enormous central square, heaving with tourists and locals dressed head to toe in white with red handkerchiefs tied around their necks, randomly erupting in cheers of 'Viva San Fermin!' It was chaotic, boisterous and disorienting. Suddenly that wave that had effortlessly carried me to a different continent crashed and everything felt foreign.

So I did what any young man in my position would—I called my mum. And Tommy's mum. Multiple times. My mum called Tommy's mum and at some point Tommy called his mum to give her an address of a nearby building, and she phoned my mum. It took two hours, but finally I had actual coordinates. I scouted the buildings lining the square and there, leaning in a doorway with his arms crossed and a sly smile on his face, was Tommy the Fly. We had been a few feet away from each other the whole time.

The Sanfermines slaughters everyone—at least metaphorically. The whole city drinks all night and runs with the bulls in the morning. It's revelry without end. On the third day, passed out in the park, waiting for our hearts to stop pounding from that morning's brush with death, we said enough and packed our bags. After a short stop in Barcelona, we'd head to the Greek Islands.

There are few places better for a young person to be than the Greek Islands in high summer. Middle-aged men might grumble that the islands have become overrun with tourists, but the young man sees only a playground of beautiful people from all over the world with sun-kissed bodies that dance from dusk to dawn. We meant to stay for a week; we ended up there for a month—and it was hard to tear ourselves away even then. Day after day we lounged in the sun, taking breaks only to swim in the clear blue Aegean Sea or pool our drachmas for some tzatziki and gyros. At night we danced and drank grappa. When someone in Santorini insisted we see the blue-domed chapels of Ios, we hopped a ferry to the party island. When another traveller told us about the spectacular sunset in Mykonos that turns the island's brown rock to gold, we moved north to yet another all-night fest. It was pure freedom, the kind you can only experience when you've got time on your side and a little cash in your pocket.

The day eventually came, in August, when we had to go. Tommy's parents had emigrated from Calabria, Italy, a few decades before, but his entire extended family—on both sides—still lived in Francavilla, and we had both promised to visit. I like to think that not much throws me, but shifting from the Greek Islands, with its shoulder-to-shoulder crowds of young bikini-clad tourists, to a village of two thousand Southern Italians certainly did.

Like many families in Francavilla, Tommy's lived in separate houses on the same plot of land. In the main house lived his eighty-year-old nonna, the matriarch, reliably dressed in black in the custom of Italian widows. An uncle and his family resided in another house and his aunt and her brood in a third. There were kids and pigs and goats and vegetables growing on every spare patch of land. As we walked up to the front door, all I could think was, What in god's name are we doing here?

The answer came soon enough: we were eating. We had arrived just in time for lunch, the largest meal of the day, an eight-course, three-hour feast during which Tommy's uncle regularly got drunk and fell asleep at the table. That first night we journeyed across town to visit Tommy's father's family. In our honour, they laid out a similar spread, though the evening meal is normally more modest. I couldn't speak a word of Italian and no one in either family except Tommy knew English, so I asked him to tell them that we had just eaten. He looked at me dumbfounded. 'I can't tell them that,' he whispered. So we ate again. Every time I would slow down, someone would ask Tommy whether I didn't like the food. By the end of it all, I felt like a foie gras goose.

The next morning I woke up late and jumped in the shower before breakfast. When I returned to my room, all of my clothes had been removed from my luggage and folded neatly or hung up in the closet. I swung around to see if my mum was there, until I remembered that not even my mum would unpack my bags. This was old-world Italy and there was no running from it.

It took four days for me to find my groove. I had got up early, rejuvenated at last from the sleep deprivation of Greece, and tiptoed downstairs to make a cup of coffee. I entered the kitchen to find three generations of women, ages twenty to eighty, rolling pasta, making sausages and preparing fresh tomato sauce. Nonna, who at full height came up to my armpit, brushed by me carrying an enormous pot of water. Someone handed me a cup of coffee, which she had made to full-bodied perfection in the *caffettiera* on the stovetop, and I sat down to watch.

It sounds crazy, but I hadn't realised until that moment that these women had crafted every bite of food I had consumed in the last three days. It hit me that the fat pig outside was destined to become the salami hanging in the larder, while the tomatoes and eggplants ripening on the vines were the same ones we would devour over handmade fusilli at lunch. These women cured their own olives and made their own goat's cheese. They planted crops and butchered livestock. One day a week, Nonna baked bread in the wood-fire oven out back. She'd stack the loaves on top of the stone wall by the front gate, and neighbours on their way by would grab a loaf and drop off whatever they had in surplus as payment. Food in Calabria was pride, self-sufficiency and community all mixed together in one mouthful.

And food was largely the work of women, with the exception of salami and wine, which the men always made. In our modern world, where fathers change diapers and women run multinational corporations, it all sounds a bit dated, if not outright sexist, to say that the women slaved away in the kitchen while the men trudged off to work. But tradition reigned supreme in southern Italy and, rather than stifling, it seemed to reflect an elegant symbiosis within the family, founded on mutual respect for what everyone brought to the table. It was the basis of their extreme closeness. You could feel the love and appreciation every time we all sat down for a meal.

What makes the people of Calabria so special is their undying appreciation, not just of food, but also of the cultivation of the ingredients that become family legacy. Neighbouring families war over who makes the best, most authentic, recipe for everything from tomato sauce to minestrone. And while the outsider may not be able to appreciate the nuance, an extra pass of the tomatoes through the mill—a technique handed down from generation to generation—makes all the difference.

After that morning, I spent a lot of time in the kitchen. The women would give me small jobs, dicing onions or slicing eggplant, and eventually I graduated to making pasta and canning enough sauce to carry them through the cold weather months. There were never any recipes to read or measuring cups to gauge the proper amount and I still didn't speak a lick of Italian. I just had to watch and follow their lead.

I literally followed the entire family's lead every night after dinner when they'd take their evening stroll through town. There wasn't much to see except a church and some villas, but sightseeing wasn't the goal. All along the path, neighbours would join us for a while, snaking throughout the group, talking about the day's news, sharing local gossip, and solving the world's problems. It makes perfect sense that the slow-food movement began in Italy. That relaxed, leisurely philosophy to cooking permeated everything they did.

Except perhaps driving. To this day, I have never ridden in a car that moved as fast as the tricked-out Alfa Romeo driven by Tommy's cousin. He was bringing us on a short holiday down the coast to Tropea, a seaside resort town built high on the cliffs overlooking the Tyrrhenian Sea. It was a 40-kilometre trip that by reasonably law-breaking speeds should have taken forty-five minutes. We got there in twenty, though my stomach didn't catch up for hours.

Compared to Francavilla, Tropea felt like a metropolis though it still had that quiet Calabria vibe. Glowing historic buildings made of gold-coloured stone lined cobblestoned streets featuring bars and clubs and eateries that served frittatas made with cipolle di Tropea, the revered local red onion. We walked the 200 stone steps from the high cliffs to the beach below and played endless matches of table soccer. At night, the clubs came alive but, unlike in the Greek Islands, the crowd was made up entirely of locals. After two days, our skin brown from lounging in the sun, we took the white-knuckle ride back to Francavilla.

Hair-raising speed has a plus side, particularly when you're itching to be somewhere. Tropea was a slender slice of paradise, but I missed the sleepy village and the people who had so graciously embraced me as one of their own. In just a few weeks, I had fallen in love with the culture of long lunches, homemade fare and family. Coming back, the question wasn't what am I doing in Francavilla, but how did the rest of the world get so far away from the Calabrian way of life?

Tommy and I would leave just after the tomato harvest to travel around Italy. But as autumn closed in, I was nearly broke, so we said goodbye and I set off for London. There, I knocked on the door of Marco Pierre White's Café Royal and offered to work for free just for the opportunity to learn from the Michelin-starred genius. I would end up staying for eight years, sweating my way from peeling potatoes to head chef and from sleeping on my mate's couch to actually having a flat. It was a wild time full of fine food, fancy dining and furious tempers. I've often said that Marco taught me everything I know about cooking, and that's true. But Francavilla taught me everything about why I wanted to cook.

GAEL GREENE was the diva of restaurant criticism as the Insatiable Critic for *New York* magazine for 40 years. Among her seven books are two best-selling erotic novels, *Blue Skies, No Candy* and *Dr. Love*, and a memoir, *Insatiable: Tales from a Life of Delicious Excess*. With the late James Beard, Greene co-founded Citymeals on Wheels in 1981 to help feed New York City's homebound elderly.

AFLOAT ON THE AMAZON

Gael Greene

Machu Picchu before my knees caved was the goal. It was a trip we'd wanted to make and postponed too long. Granted, I would be the last kid on my block to do the Inca tour. Was there a must-see not everyone had done yet?

We are persuaded to start tropical on an Amazon cruise. Don't tell anyone, please, but I thought the Amazon was in Brazil. The consulting chef from Lima will be on board to tell us about Amazon products. Okay, digging out malaria pills.

Ten days before departure I get a call. The boat has been robbed by bandits. 'It never happened before,' our agent notes. 'It will never happen again. No one was hurt. The police are patrolling. The government won't let them threaten tourism.'

At dinner that night our Fodor writer pal Harry fills us in. 'It's not bandits you need to worry about,' says Harry. 'It's panthers. And tarantulas. You need a tarantula whistle to scare them off.' He suggests I call Hammacher Schlemmer.

Two days before takeoff for Lima, a very chastened travel agent calls. The boat has been robbed by bandits again. It seems they took everything: money, of course, credit cards, watches and jewelry, computers, cell phones, iPods, even couturier clothes.

'Where were the police?' I ask. 'Didn't you say it couldn't happen again?'

'It was foggy and the bandits came up on the other side. The police couldn't see. The trip has been cancelled.'

Next day she calls again: 'We just heard from a couple we couldn't reach yesterday because they were at a conference in Chile. They still want to go. Are you game?'

Our contact insists, contrary to news reports, no one was bound or gagged in the robbery. I have been bound but never gagged. Wish I were younger. Been wishing that a lot lately.

In Lima our hotel, the Country Club, loans us a suite so we can shower and repack before we fly to Iquitos to board the boat. We've slept through the entire flight on LAN's stretch-out beds. Ambien sleeping tabs, just to be sure. We will check Lima dress-up baggage here, and repack hiking boots and tropical gear. I've never gone anywhere completely naked of jewelry before. Steven is deciding what camera he can live without. We leave everything we can't afford to lose—passports, credit cards, big cash, computer, telephones, two cameras, my precious green ombre pashmina—in the Aqua Expeditions office safe and take $200 in Peruvian solas to stash in our room safe—no sense being killed by bandits enraged at finding nothing worth stealing. I'm so paranoid now I even worry that my silver Tiffany taxi whistle might scare away tarantulas in the rainforest and attract a panther.

Our boat looks like a floating motel from afar but up close it's definitely five star, with a staff of twenty-two at our service, tented deck, a library of books in the bar, and a vast king-size bed with poufy comforter facing a sweep of window in our air-conditioned suite. We meet our fellow passengers, the fearless duo, Whit and Jill. He's career army. She's a perfect army wife. Travels cheerfully. Carries a complete medic kit. 'We are both expert shots,' she assures me. 'If they give us guns, we can take care of any bandits.'

The buffet lunch that first day is Italian but, afterward, consulting chef Pedro Miguel Schiaffino, slight and slim in khakis, assures me that I am eating Amazon potatoes and shrimp from a nearby river. Schiaffino, a Culinary Institute of America alum, did a master's in Italian restaurants, before becoming fired up with fusing Andean and rainforest products and European technique with a passion that is contagious.

In our first afternoon exploring the Amazon with our guides (with no other guests, two of them are sharing us), Steven catches a piranha and then tosses it back. So does everyone else. I'm not into birds. But Whit and Jill are. Each of us has been given a small booklet to check off whatever mammal, reptile, bird or insect we see and I'm hopelessly competitive. Jill is almost as beady-eyed as the guides who see White-headed Marsh Tyrants where I see only bark and leaves. I take their word for Cobalt-winged Parakeet,

Lineated Woodpecker, Yellow-rumped Cacique, and check them off. Pretty soon I'm seeing spider monkeys and Masked Crimson Tanagers too. Well, something red flew by. And no way could I miss the thrill of pink dolphins leaping into the air and splashing all around the boat. One evening the guides bring mimosas to serve at sunset with plantain chips before we set off in search of nocturnal critters. Usiel captures a caiman lizard, holding its snout tight shut while he lectures and checks to see if it has a two-pronged penis—no, it's just a female. Just.

We are served Brazilian nut soup, star-fruit chutney with a beef brochette and deep-fried yucca beignets with ice cream made from the palm fruit, *aguaje*. When the guide, Riccardo, swears we will not encounter a malaria mosquito anywhere on our itinerary, I quit the dreaded medication. To celebrate I order a pisco sour; one night I have two. I complain to Pedro Miguel that the dinner menus are boring: too often beef or catfish. 'The catfish is local,' he says, defending the on-board dining crew. 'Well, maybe it is too safe,' he agrees. The company is more concerned about frightening fussy eaters than about gourmandlich fantasies.

I'm happiest with the native touches in the lunch buffet. Star-fruit vinaigrette. Steamed vegetables, not all of them recognizable. Roasted pork with particularly tangy pineapple. Deep-fried won tons filled with chicken and pork in a *camu camu* sauce. A rainforest fruit the size of a large grape with a purplish red skin, also known as rumberry; it is supposedly one of the world's richest sources of vitamin C.

Fresh hearts of palm are a rare delicacy for us in a soufflé and also in a salad with a vinaigrette of *cocona* at Tuesday's 'Amazon Lunch'. Pedro Miguel breaks one of the yellow plum-like fruits open to show us the pulp, and says it's related to tomatoes and eggplants, high in niacin, used in juice, ice cream, sorbet and jams or mixed with chili peppers for a hot sauce. There are local river snails, with sweet pepper salsa, local beans, grilled plantains, and fresh water prawns wrapped in mysterious local leaves. Look up cashew at Rain-tree.com and its alleged curative powers are astonishing. I am not that impressed with white chocolate mousse. But then I'm no fan of white chocolate in any iteration. Tuesday's tangy camu camu tart is more like it. The *huito* flavoring the semifreddo (with Brazilian guava sauce) is also used medicinally or is cooked with sugar to make a preserve and comes from a tree Amazon natives climb to gather palm fruit.

A soaking rain our last day washes out plans to visit a small local market with Pedro Miguel. I'm cranky, wondering why we waited till the last minute. But then criss-crossing Peru over the next ten days, we linger in a dozen markets—our canny guide quickly realizes that we're hooked on markets more than poets' graves or ancient amphitheaters. One Sunday we visit a bread-baking town outside of Cuzco, then a pit stop devoted to guinea pigs from roadside ovens and a few miles away, *chicharrónes* heaven, a village where seemingly everyone on either side of the road hawks fried pork rinds.

Back in Lima we catch up with the chef at Malabar, the upscale restaurant he opened with his parents—their collections of Venetian glass, Japanese porcelain, African sculpture and contemporary art give the place a living-room feel. At the bar with our new best friend and guide, pisco brewer Guillermo Ferreyros, I discover I prefer my pisco sour 'dry'—it's headier, more tangy, not so aggressively sweet.

I don't need to know the chef is a pioneer of exploiting the diversity of Peruvian ingredients to revel in his world-class cooking. But I imagine that American locavores will be impressed. Pedro Miguel's mastery is on display, beginning with the nuts and seeds cooked in *Sacha Inchi* oil from the Amazon that he sends out as an amuse, the exotic fruit sauces, and an impressive array of house-baked breads. As a critic, I must taste each one. As an undisciplined eater, I ask for seconds of the nutted purple cornbread. His tataki of *chita*, a rockfish, scattered with leek green and chicharrón dust has been 'cooked' with lime. Peru has no lemons. 'Lime is our lemon,' the chef explains. The black scallops from the north in the risotto are allegedly aphrodisiacal. Exquisitely rolled spaghetti in a Parmesan foam hides nuggets of red-wine baked pigeon and duck foie gras. That could be aphrodisiacal too. The crackling skin of suckling pig plays against smoked eggplant and plaintain puree. A spring roll of custardy cherimoya fruit with mandarin juice, black mint and a sorbet of *hierba buena* is the dessert I remember.

Steven asks for a Lima market tour. It is drizzling when we get to the wholesale fish stalls after bouncing over unpaved streets in the chef's banged-up truck. Pedro Miguel gives us a primer on what we're seeing, stopping to hug friends, or introduce us to a crab we've never seen before. In one corner he points out tables of Amazon seaweed and a woman specializing in rainforest products with the offhand air of a father playing down the exploits of a brilliant child. Himself in this case. His passionate use of indigenous products has inspired other chefs. Not far away in the Mercado Mayorista de Frutas, he marvels that strawberries are huge and ripe and any fruit can be found even out of season. He points out tree tomatoes, tomatillos, 'very good pecans', soursop and monster pineapples. He sips sugar-cane juice from a cart pressing the stalks, and drops some plums from a friend's display into my tote. 'It's the season for cherimoya,' he notes. Passing a truck unloading crates. We watch two women polishing limes with a shoe brush to make them shiny. 'Now is watermelon season in the Amazon,' he observes. 'Want to stop by a neighborhood market?' he asks. Yes, we would. But we need to get back to the hotel to dress for an earlyish lunch so we'll be hungry again when it's time for dinner. Our pisco-maker friend is determined to show us the best places in the four days that I plotted for sophisticated eating. Lima, it seems, is on its way to becoming a city of restless and demanding foodies. I can cross Machu Picchu off our must list but I know I'll be going back to Lima one day soon for its annual fall food festival. It didn't exist in 2009 when I tasted the new inventions of gifted chefs in an early contagion. But now it does.

RITA MAE BROWN is the author of the iconic novel *Rubyfruit Jungle*. An Emmy-nominated screenwriter and a poet, she lives in Afton, Virginia, in the foothills of the Blue Ridge Mountains, where she is an avid fox hunter and is master of her Fox Hunt Club.

WHAT BECOMES A LADY

Rita Mae Brown

Until about the last forty years of the twentieth century even small towns published a morning paper and an evening paper, each one representing a different point of view. Dad insisted I read the editorial page in each paper. At the dinner table he would ask my opinion. After I answered, mother often quipped, 'That might be too much opinion.'

To even be allowed to eat at the dinner table with the adults was a rite of passage. Children ate in the kitchen until they proved they could use the utensils and, more importantly, be silent. To be asked something at the table was a sign you were growing up.

By the time I was ten, I had mastered what I could say as well as learning that sometimes what you don't say is as important as what you do. That dinner table was training for what lay beyond.

Once a year, Mother (Juts) and Louise (Wheezie) would call on their cousin, Hazel Bowater, who lived in splendor on Philadelphia's Main Line. Could I last the five hours' drive due north without wrinkling my outfit? If I didn't move, yes. As I rocked in the back of Aunt Wheezie's big butt car, hood looming into next week, I reviewed which fork to use, which glass held what beverage and how to look interested when I was anything but.

Mother and Aunt Wheezie, glowing in pastels, hat, shoes and purse matching, took turns driving. If that person behind the wheel was Aunt Wheezie I held the side of the back seat. Wheezie believed in acceleration.

When we finally arrived at the impressive stone mansion, I walked up the winding path between the two sisters who looked alike as twins.

'Remember, no matter what is placed in front of you, give it a brave try. And smile,' Aunt Wheezie counseled.

'And don't pick on Gallatin.' Mother paused. 'He's not as forward as you are.' She turned to her older sister. 'How's my lipstick?'

'Joan Crawford divine.' Aunt Wheezie's gaze fell on me. 'Hazel will look at you with the searching eye. Hear?'

'Yes, ma'am.'

Aunt Wheezie lived in fear that I would reveal her relentless efforts to render me feminine a failure.

We knocked on the door. Bixby, the portly butler, opened it.

'Julia Ellen and Louise.' He smiled, a genuine smile. 'And your precious little girl.'

'Semi-precious,' mother shot back.

Laughing, Bixby ushered us into a sitting room filled with eighteenth-century furniture. The only reason I knew that was Aunt Hazel (how she allowed me to address her) had been telling me since I was six.

Hazel Bowater stood to greet her cousins. The three women, good-looking, trim, all with deep, wavy hair, were clearly related. Hazel wore a pale green spring day dress with a thin trim of feathers along the low neckline. Like everything she had it was beautiful.

Gallatin smiled at me, offering his hand so we sat apart from the adults though we could hear them.

'Juts, that child is too brown. You don't want her looking like a field hand.'

'She's in the sun a lot.' Mother slid away from an argument.

'Do you still play baseball?' Gallatin asked.

'Sure.'

'I play first base. We don't allow girls to play.' He breathed in. 'It's a boys school but we still wouldn't allow girls to play if it wasn't.'

'If we go outside I'll throw the ball further than you do,' I bragged, but knew I could back it up.

He leaned toward me. 'Mother won't allow it. She says competition is vulgar, unless it's at school, of course.'

Hazel rose and we moved into the dining room, flowers everywhere and the long table set with luncheon china. Every time of the day had a special set of china, and silver too.

It seemed like hours between the cold soup and the next course.

I crossed my eyes at Gallatin. He giggled loudly, which drew an icy stare from his mother, who then turned her full attention to my mother.

'Julia, why are you wearing that overlarge aquamarine in the broad of day?'

Mother grinned, wiggling her finger, 'It always reminds me of your Aunt Mimi, my mother.'

Telling Hazel my grandmother's name irritated her but she pushed it back, forcing a smile.

Ever adroit when she wanted to be, Aunt Wheezie glided into the conversation. 'Hazel, which of your mother's jewels do you like the best?'

Beaming, she said, 'The three strands of pearls that hang below my waist. Every time I wear them my handsome George says I look like the girl he married. He's so busy, you know, on the train to New York at least once a week. You know, George gets calls daily at the brokerage house from Boston, Chicago, even San Francisco. Such a gift for finance that he has to work long hours just to satisfy others, guide them. Everyone wants to know what George Bowater thinks.' She paused, then sighed. 'He works much too hard. I try to tell him to slow down but you girls know how that goes. You can't tell them anything.'

'We know.' Aunt Wheezie laughed.

Mother, sensitive to children, asked Gallatin, 'Have you thought about what you'd like to do when you grow up?'

'Paint.' His face lit up. 'I want to be a painter.'

Hazel gave a high, thin laugh. 'Darling boy, the Bowater men leave that to the lower orders. You will follow in your father's illustrious footsteps.'

'Yes, Mother.'

That was the only remark addressed to Gallatin.

None to me.

When the crème brûlée was cleared from the table, the ladies strolled in the symmetrical garden, lilacs in full bloom.

Gallatin and I walked a distance behind them.

'If you get your baseball, we can see who's the best.'

He shook his head, saying nothing.

⇢⊁⊱

Driving the long way home, the sisters, having fulfilled their annual obligation, chattered with relief and glee.

'She wants Momma's ring.'

'Juts, she always wanted that ring from the time we were kids. The woman could buy an entire jewelry store but she longs for that aquamarine.' Aunt Wheezie added, 'Hazel always wants what she can't have.'

'George never comes for lunch. At least not when we're there.'

'He goes to his club. And what do you think about that story of him going up to New York all the time?' Aunt Wheezie said with a shrug.

'Same as you, I think.'

'And that feather trim on her dress. Egret?'

'Vulture,' mother replied.

Aunt Wheezie, laughing hard, choked out, 'Hazel believes her décolleté is a Philadelphia treasure.'

'George no longer does.'

This sent the two of them into peals of laughter. They delighted themselves while I thought about solemn Gallatin. He really wanted to chuck that baseball. He wanted to show me up. Course, I could snap him like a twig but I liked him anyway.

'Mother?'

'What, Semi?'

'Oh, Mom.' I rolled my eyes, which she could see as she was looking in the rear-view mirror.

'What, shortcakes?'

'Did you like the crème brûlée?'

'Yes. Hazel has the best cook in three states. Tell you what, it's worth a five-hour trip to boredom.'

'Those raspberries, the raspberry sauce on the crème brûlée,' Aunt Wheezie sighed with significance. 'Heaven.'

We rode a bit more and I asked, 'Mother, why is Aunt Hazel like that?'

A long pause followed this then finally my mother answered. 'Because all she has is money.'

MONIQUE TRUONG is the author of two novels, *Bitter in the Mouth* and *The Book of Salt*. She lives in Brooklyn, New York, but can often be found elsewhere in the world.

ENCHANTED ISLE

Monique Truong

The emotional equivalence of jet lag is the end of a love affair and yet you, foolish and besotted lover, won't let go. You're still keeping time by his sun and moon, waking when he wakes, and sleeping only when he closes his eyes. Travel, when it was slow, used to provide a halfway house of sorts—a neither here nor there—for the recently expelled and broken-hearted. On the ship or the long locomotive journey back home, the traveler had time to consider the landscape of where she had been and to comprehend how her body, with every minute and hour, was now deliberately moving farther and farther away. By the time that she has reached home, the traveler has had days or weeks to understand the absence of that other body of land, to hold her heart steady, and her head high again. Air travel changed everything.

We now allow ourselves to be propelled there and back with such great speed that when we return our bodies protest, rebel, seeking something, concrete or intangible, that we can no longer offer. No wonder our bodies punish us with unrequited sleeplessness and crushing fatigue.

My worst and most prolonged bouts of jet lag haven't always correlated with the distances traveled or the differences in time. Often, the intensity of my stupor has everything to do with how hard I had fallen. Like love for a man or a woman, love for a destination on a map cannot be planned. Sometimes, the affection is hard earned, even a result of a feat of courage or a trial by ordeal. Once in a while, if fate and luck travels with me, there's a singular, indelible moment that feels like a first kiss.

On Lefkada, one of the Ionian Islands off the western coast of Greece, the kiss took place on an open patio with a sweeping view of the foothills of Mt. Stavrota, interrupted only by the occasional columns of swaying cypress trees. The scent of Lefkada in the late spring was courtesy of the ginestra flowers, which bloomed bright yellow and covered the island in patches, like sunlight. They released a delicious fragrance: crushed fresh herbs—mint, thyme, fennel fronds, sage and oregano—with a dollop of clover honey on top, and laced with the improbable, mouthwatering scent of a butter cake that's almost ready to be taken out of the oven.

I had traveled to Lefkada to research the Greek-Irish writer Lafcadio Hearn, the subject of my novel-in-progress. From 1850 till his passing in 1904, Hearn made his home on three continents. Lefkada, also the name of the island's main town, was Hearn's birthplace and namesake, and for me a necessary portal into this man's peripatetic life.

You must believe me that the following is fact and not mere puffery: from its inception, a novel is an act of courage. It does not always require the author to travel, but it's always a long journey into the pitch darkness for her. Only the brave or, perhaps, the foolish will dare it.

I arrived on Lefkada in the early hours of the morning after a very long travel day. After our plane touched down in Athens, my husband and I inched across the city in a taxi—actually, it felt more like we inched around the city, as in an unbargained-for full circle of Athens—only to arrive at the bus station to find that our seat reservations had been given away by a taciturn bus dispatcher whose English language skills fluctuated between shoulder shrugs and monosyllabic grunts. This man had gifted our reservations away as though they were roses or a box of chocolates. Our faces, ashen and fallen, didn't hide our grief. Some of the boarding passengers, probably the ones who had received our reservations, felt sorry for us and explained in fluent English that the next bus for Lefkada was in five hours. Resignation, dejection and exhaustion immediately set in. We headed to the bus station's cafeteria, where those three stages of travel grief seemed to have afflicted everyone present. Small children with doleful eyes asked us again and again if we wanted to buy little packets of tissue paper from them. I think they knew that I wanted to cry.

During the summer months, it's possible to reach Lefkada from Athens via a short plane ride. In May, however, the Aktion National Airport was still closed. Lefkada is connected to the mainland of Greece by a bridge, so the options were a five-hour bus ride or a rental car. Driving in Greece seemed like an invitation to tragedy to me, so we opted for the bus, which was instead an invitation to prolonged boredom and acute moments of heart-in-the-throat terror because there was something even worse than driving in Greece (as our taxi ride had just shown us): being driven by a Greek driver in Greece. Somehow this simple fact had eluded me when we were making our plans.

When we finally boarded the Lefkada-bound bus, a modern behemoth that was again woefully overbooked, I watched from my coveted seat as the dyspeptic dispatcher turned away would-be passengers. I felt sorry for them all, especially an old man with cheeks so sunken that they seemed like the basins of a dried-out sea, but I was also thrilled that I would soon be getting closer to Hearn's island.

The sun was already starting its descent as our bus, like a towering cruise ship, slowly navigated Athen's rush hour traffic. Gilded and then rose-hued, gridlock had never looked so sublime. By the time the congestion spat our bus out onto the national highway, somber purples and blues cloaked the ribbons of asphalt ahead of us. Then began the cluster of hours when I could have been on any highway, almost anywhere in the world. The visual boredom that only modernity and its generic throughways can engender, I thought as the bus sped us southward.

Soon though, I would long for those steady, dependable and nondescript arteries because during the latter half of the journey the bus, devolving into a lumbering giant, would cling onto roads so narrow and exuberantly pocked that I was certain that it was sharing them with goats. The headlights of the bus allowed for just enough illumination to show us passengers, who were unwise enough to look, how very near to a plunging death we were. A shoulder wasn't to be seen for many kilometers. A slip of the hand, an involuntary twitch even, and the bus and the awaiting cliffs would meet in a matter of seconds. When Hearn left Lefkada for Dublin, he did so via ship and he never returned. It was becoming apparent to me why. To reach his island, you have to be brave or foolish, which is really differentiated only by a sliver of motivation in the face of utter ignorance.

The scheduled five-hour bus trip was, in fact, seven hours. There were stops at every small village or suggestion of a village from the moment that the bus crossed onto the island till it reached Lefkada town. The discharge of passengers into the nightscape of single-story houses with carports draped in grapevines, lit by the occasional gray-white light of an outdoor bulb, was quick enough, but it was locating each passenger's luggage that caused significant delay. These travelers—one per village was the apparent allotment—seemed to have all brought back with them a large chunk of Athens, wrapped in odd-shaped packages or stuffed into bulging woven plastic tote bags, which were difficult to distinguish and to extract from the bowels of the idling beast. We, onboard, could only stare haplessly as the passenger below shook his or her head, denying ownership of what had been pulled out before eventually grabbing onto something large and unwieldy with both hands and heading finally home.

Our journey ended at an otherwise deserted parking lot in Lefkada town. My husband called the owners of the inn where we were booked, and they came to pick us up in a jeep. We loaded our luggage and squeezed in for the short ride to the inn, during which my husband was coherent enough to describe our travel woes while I wished that I had purchased a packet of tissues from one of those melancholic but enterprising children. They were silent little soothsayers: *Oh, lady, you'll need these tissues before the night's end!*

Located on the second floor, our room was dominated by a white four-poster bed, which was much more inviting than the hospital beds that I thought we would be in. The room also had a set of French doors that opened onto a small balcony half hidden by the branches and waxy leaves of a rubber tree, whose roots were in the courtyard below. I opened the French doors, and we lay on the bed, speechless and exhausted. Then, as a welcoming salvo or a mean-spirited lullaby, we heard the sound that would become familiar to us in the nights to come: the insistent thump thump, thump thump of dance music leaking from the town's nightclubs and bars.

The bridge that so helpfully connects the mainland to this island also has cursed it and now us. Lefkada is the 'easy' island getaway for mainland Greeks as well as the Europeans and Brits who used it for bachelor parties and other modern rites of loud, obnoxious debaucheries. Hearn, an admirer of ancient cultures and the subtleties of the natural world, would have rolled over in his grave. I rolled over in our massive bed, exhausted to the bone, wondering why I had followed a dead writer to his desecrated, spoilt birthplace.

I slept the rest of that day away, our bed a raft on a calm sea. I awoke to the sound of birds attacking something tasty among the glossy leaves of the rubber tree. The flapping of their wings and their high-pitched squawks were both gleeful and terrifying, the precise combination that made them such perfect vessels for the uncanny. I thought of Hearn, whose chosen totem was the raven because of his admiration for Edgar Allen Poe and for the heightened intelligence that these birds possess. In lieu of a signature, Hearn would often end his notes with a winsome doodle of a raven. My next thought was whether the flock of its cousins outside my window was a sign: that Hearn had decided to accompany me home or, perhaps, he was just in absentia mocking me.

We spent the following day exploring Lefkada town's historical center, which boasted a fishbone-shaped street plan, dating back to when the Venetians shortly ruled this island from 1502 to 1503. Now, the pedestrian-only streets along the central square were lined with shops that offered the universal tourist trappings: scarves and jewelry from India, subpar gelato stands, outdoor cafes where French fries and hamburgers could be ordered but shouldn't be. I was surprised not to hear the ubiquitous strains of the Peruvian pan flutes being played by a trio with CDs for sale. Lefkada town's saving graces, literally, were its diminutive churches, with their plain, stoic and timeworn facades, dating from the seventeenth and eighteenth centuries. They each looked like a sepia-toned photograph.

Despite what we had previously and wisely agreed not to do, the next morning my husband and I rented a car from the inn. We needed to get out of Lefkada town, and the only way to do so was via car or bicycle. The island of Lefkada has a mountain range smack in the middle of it, so to get from Lefkada town down to the southern tip of the island meant a straight ascent and then descent. Of course, this perverse island would require us to go up in order to go down. My husband consulted the map, spoke with the owners of the inn, who told us about a little restaurant in the mountains that would be open for lunch, and we were off!

Unfortunately, the map of Lefkada, town and island, was drawn by fabulists. We became our own Greek taxi driver, circumnavigating the town until we finally found the elusive road out of the fish bone. Within minutes we were in the countryside, and I rolled down the window and unwittingly took in my first lungful of ginestra-scented air. I immediately felt hopeful. I would later read that in aromatherapy ginestra is used for treating depression and co-dependency. Perhaps that's why I also felt no guilt whatsoever about leaving all thoughts of Hearn and his birthplace behind me. I hadn't even located the house where he was born yet, but Lefkada town, you were bringing me down.

Our car, meanwhile, was desperately trying to get us up the two-lane mountain roads. The inn's Smart Car had apparently never left the sea-level topography of Lefkada town. There was no power and no acceleration for the sharp inclines, and no shifting of the gears could remedy it. My husband was an excellent, resourceful driver, but

the Smart Car had defeated him. We found ourselves
stalled out and then rolling backward, as oncoming
cars swerved and passed us without a reduction in their
speed. I screamed each time. He told me that didn't help.
I screamed anyhow, and we were on our way to an all-out
fight. No amount of ginestra was going to help us now.
After two more near-death experiences—the passing
drivers honking and displaying colorful hand gestures—we
decided that the Smart Car was a profoundly dumb idea
and headed back into town. The Smart Car performed
excellently downhill. My husband and I did not. Our fight
had spiraled, and I used it as a catchall for every one of my
recent travel grievances, disappointments and despairs. He,
of course, wasn't the cause of any of them, just my unlucky
companion.

Maybe the ginestra had indeed kicked in again because
once we had arrived back in town we silently decided—
because we weren't talking to each other at this point—that
we would not be beaten by this island. We rented what we
hoped would be a proper car, the inauspiciously named Fiat
Panda. What was more plodding and unmotivated than a
panda? The Fiat Sloth?

In our Panda, we clambered up those same mountain
roads with relative ease. I suppose 'plodding and
unmotivated' could be also framed as sure and steady. I was
speaking to my husband again. I was also sticking my head
out the car window, dog-like, and taking in giant gulps of the
intoxicating Lefkadan air. I was even beginning to forgive
Hearn for his inconvenient entry point into this world.

We were on our way to the day's next and most important goal: a late lunch. The inn owners had given us a description of a small restaurant that was a page right out of my wish book: located in a remote mountain village, owned by a couple—she's the chef and he's the host and server— offering Greek dishes but with a twist because the owners are British, and the garden that they tended provided much of the restaurant's vegetables and greens. Even its name, the Katoghi, made me think of the appellation for a small, elegant sailing ship.

But first, we needed to find the village of Vafkeri, which according to the fabulists was where we had driven past, circled round, and driven past yet again. We stopped the Panda, and my husband and I stared at the mountainside, willing Vafkeri to appear, like a magic door. It didn't. Instead, we followed the road farther up the mountain, took a turn that was clearly not indicated on the map, and there it was: a small sign that promised Vafkeri. We were now operating on faith. The Panda and faith were all that we had to rely upon. We were on a mountain and hungry. It was an age-old story in these parts, except for the Panda.

The road to Vafkeri led us to a sign for the Katoghi, which indicated that the remaining 50 meters there would need to be traversed on foot. I looked at my watch and was filled with the dread of a tried and true pessimist: what if the restaurant were closed? What if we had traveled all this way—from New York City, for God's sake!—only to be turned away? The longest 50 meters of my life ended on the terrace with the spectacular view.

We were greeted by Peter. We knew his name immediately because he offered it to us. He chatted with us like we were old friends who had dropped by his ridiculously scenic property for a bite to eat. He told us that Alison had made a delicious courgette tart that afternoon and that there were still a couple of pieces left, and dessert included a lemon mousse. I think I heard all the gods singing at that moment.

My husband and I spent many hours on the Katoghi's terrace. We watched as Alison walked into the garden and snipped a bowlful of greens and herbs for our salads. We ate the fresh, simple fare that she sent out of her kitchen. We talked with Peter about why they had ventured from Suffolk to Lefkada, and why I had come there as well. I told him about Hearn and why this writer, who had traveled by necessity from Greece to Ireland to the United States, and then by euphoric free will to Japan, was to me a compelling example of personal and creative reinvention.

Before we reluctantly left, I made sure that we took photographs of the terrace, the view, and of ourselves. I wanted to document and to remember where following Lafcadio Hearn had taken us. Hearn's island at that moment, lit by a late afternoon sun, did feel to me like a kiss but not on the lips or even on the cheeks. Lefkada's kiss was on the forehead, a blessing for traveling without a map, guided by the impossible desire to trace the steps of some other soul, and finding your own way out of the metaphorical dark.

As for the jet lag, it's two years later and I'm still writing my Hearn novel, which means that I'm still keeping time by his sun and moon.

JOE DUNTHORNE was born in 1982, brought up in Swansea, and now lives in London. His debut novel, *Submarine*, has been adapted for the big screen and was released to critical acclaim in 2011. His stories, poems and journalism have been published in the *Guardian, The New York Times Magazine*, *Independent*, *Financial Times* and *Sunday Times* in the U.K. His second novel, *Wild Abandon*, was published in 2011.

THEY EAT MAGGOTS, DON'T THEY?

Joe Dunthorne

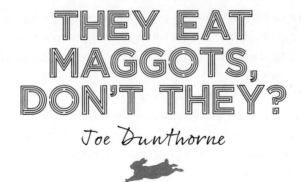

Sebastiano brought out the cauldron. He did not speak English but was able to communicate that, even if he were fluent in our language, he would still not tell us what we were about to eat. It was a surprise. He was excited. My girlfriend and I were sharing a table with an Italian couple and their two young boys who came to Sebastiano's farm in the mountains of Sardinia every year for their holidays. They knew what was in the cauldron. The little boys wriggled in their seats with anticipation.

The mother of the family asked Sebastiano something and pointed at the cauldron. We listened to his mellifluous Italian and enjoyed his long arms covered in wiry black hair, his fine, almost lupine nose and alert eyes. He fulfilled a certain stereotype by being expressive with his hands: stirring the air, making a crumbling action with his fingertips, then drawing his hand down his own chest as though unzipping a jacket. The family cooed. Although we understood next to nothing of what he was saying, there was one word that stuck out: *'coaguli'*.

We thought of ourselves as brave eaters. Back at home in London, we were glad there was finally something in British cooking to be proud of—nose-to-tail eating—and we had been indulging ourselves in the zeitgeist: baking veal bone marrow, frying brains, roasting tongues. Although we told ourselves that the motivation for such cooking was ethical—a desire to let nothing go to waste—there was no denying that part of the appeal was macho. Who could work a bone saw? Who could boil a pig's head? Who could endure the intestinal stench of andouillette? And if you google any list of weird or frightening foods, you are sure to find one of Sardinia's famous delicacies, *casu marzu* aka maggot cheese. It's a kind of pecorino into which fly larvae have been introduced. The cheese moves beyond fermentation into decomposition. The digestive action of the larvae breaks down the fats, leaving a very soft texture, liquid in parts. Wikipedia notes that the worms can jump up to fifteen centimetres in the air and advises eye protection.

When we arrived in Sardinia, we couldn't see it on any menus. We wondered if it was one of those things—like jellied eels in London—that gets name-dropped a lot but few people actually eat. It wasn't until we met Sebastiano that we felt sure we had a man who would know. Although his farm, Testone, is located in an isolated cork forest on a tabletop mountain, people travel there for his cooking. Even the local cinghiale—wild boars—came snuffling to his back door to be fed. Pretty much everything he served while we stayed was homemade: pasta, salami, pecorino, grappa, pistachios, yoghurt, honey. On our first night, he made us unforgettable homemade ravioli and lung ragu. On our second night, he brought out the cauldron.

If it was full of maggot cheese then perhaps we had overstated our culinary fearlessness. He dunked his ladle and poured us each a bowl of dark lumpy soup the colour and texture of raspberry jam. No visible larvae. It smelled rich and we were told to spread a little on the flat bread they eat everywhere in Sardinia. It's sometimes called *carta da musica:* music paper. We were also advised to go slow, a recommendation that the two small boys—who both took a glass of grappa with their meals—cheerfully ignored. They soon had ruby-coloured stains around their mouths like badly applied lipstick. Then they resembled young vampires, gore dripping down their chins. Finally, their napkins looked as though they'd been used to staunch a wound. We saw Sebastiano watching our reactions—smiling—his teeth stained red. Could we guess the secret ingredient?

Well, it looked like blood, smelled like blood—was it blood?

Sebastiano would neither confirm nor deny. But since we had loved everything he had cooked up to that point, and since we had little or no choice in the matter, we got started, trying not to think of the lumps as clots. I took a bite, waited for fangs to replace my incisors but instead, there was the richness of, yes, blood but also onion (the lumps) and all shot through with mint. It was silky and heartening and it raised the pulse.

As we ate, Sebastiano explained—with the help of the Italian family for extra sign language—that it was called *sanguinaccio*. As well as the ingredients we'd detected, he'd crumbled in his homemade pecorino and thickened it with bread. Animal noises established that he had slaughtered a lamb that morning. This was the meal he always made when he had fresh lamb's blood.

It's not legal to buy blood over the counter in Britain because it needs to be eaten within twenty-four hours, and carefully prepared. Even in Italy, a 1992 law banned the sale of blood in some regions, which is why many people have to get it from their own animals.

By the end of the meal, all our napkins were props for B movies. Sebastiano was delighted. There was a sense that the bond you make while sharing blood soup is a bond that lasts. The youngest son of the family drew a smiley face in gore on his plate. As the evening went on, we gathered from the Italian family that we had seen nothing compared to the food Sebastiano served for parties in his huge feasting hall. Judging by their facial expressions and hand gestures, these meals were a mix between a medieval victory banquet and that scene where the blood pours out of the elevator in *The Shining.*

This all made a lasting impression. I was writing my second novel, *Wild Abandon,* at the time. It is set on a communal farm (albeit in Wales, not Sardinia) and I ended up using blood soup (disguised as tomato) as a vital motor for the plot. My girlfriend, meanwhile, was now determined that we should track down the maggot cheese.

On the last few days of our holiday, we asked around but no luck. The locals all knew about it but restaurants didn't serve it. We flew back to London and I might have given up had it not been for my girlfriend's single-mindedness. She rang one of the few Sardinian restaurants in London, Mediterranea, a low-key but well-loved spot in Crystal Palace, and spoke to the owner.

'I was wondering, do you by any chance have casu marzu?'

A pause on the line. 'Do you mean maggot cheese?'

'Yes.'

Another pause. 'Well, it's not on the menu but if you want I could bring some from my fridge at home?'

We arrived at the restaurant and my girlfriend confirmed her identity. They had been waiting for us. They gave us a special table. By special I mean it avoided the sight-lines of the rest of the customers. The food was tremendous but it could not distract us from giggly anticipation of our secret, final course. The owner emerged from the kitchen, looking furtive, carrying a shoebox-sized Tupperware close to his chest. He put it down on the table between us. He asked us to try to be subtle.

When he took the lid off, I suppose I was expecting more horror. It was not like peering into the industrial bins behind our flat. In fact, it looked fairly normal. It was a pale, crumbly cheese, almost cottaged, with a strong smell. The owner picked up my fork and dug into one of the larger cheese clouds, which disintegrated at his prodding. His eyebrows spoke of revelation.

'You're very lucky,' he said. 'They're active.'

We peered in closer and saw the maggots were not the fat squirmers you see in films. They were, in essence, made entirely of cheese. No wonder they were so well camouflaged in their surroundings. They looked like tiny pale strings and they leapt, for freedom or for joy, who could say.

He gave us each a portion to spread on flat bread and we were advised, again: go slow. He told us that his children loved this cheese, particularly the pleasure of chasing the maggots across the table before sending them to their doom. There was no question, by the way, of not eating the maggots. They were the cheese and the cheese was them, plus they were too small to really pick around. Occasionally we had to herd one or two back to our plates, if they made a rush for the border. The cheese tasted like an extremely strong, very fine blue but its greatest attribute was its texture: a mix of melting and crumbling and gooey. The owner seemed pleased with our response as he carefully resealed the Tupperware and took the maggots home.

There's a popular parenting book at the moment called *French Children Don't Throw Food*. If my girlfriend and I ever have kids, we will have higher expectations than that. Perhaps one day there will be another parenting manual: *Italian Children Taunt Maggots and Drink Blood*.

ANDRÉ ACIMAN was born in Alexandria, Egypt, and is an American memoirist, essayist, novelist, and distinguished professor of Comparative Literature at the CUNY Graduate Center. His work has appeared in *The New Yorker*, *The New York Review of Books*, *The New York Times*, and *The New Republic*. His most recent novel is *Harvard Square*.

LAST SUPPER IN TUSCANY

André Aciman

Our farmhouse in Italy was a disaster that summer. We arrived, as we'd done the years before, expecting the usual fare of miracles: the rolling hills of Tuscany, the scented groves of Umbria, the lush overripe figs of Romagna aching to drop into your palm if you so much as stared at them with lust in your eyes. The pine tree alleys leading to palaces that haven't lost a stone in centuries; sunflowers watching your every step as you thread your way between them ever so warily, patting each one on the head so it wouldn't bite or think you've trespassed. And who could forget the wines: of Montalcino, of Montepulciano, of Montecarlo, Montecucco, Monteregio, and Montescudaio—the sheer names of these hilltop towns, with their central little piazzas and their maze of lanes that keep spinning and, when you've given up hoping to find your car again, lead right into the piazza you thought you'd lost forever. Magic!

I couldn't wait to be back. We had visited Tuscany the year before with a couple, and before that with another couple, and rented a different house for a week each time. We knew the drill. Every child selects a bed—first come, first served— mom and dad get the big bed, no sitting on the couch with your sandals on, don't drink from the faucet, and easy with showers: hot water is rationed here. Above all, each son has his color-coded suitcase. Close it once you've removed what you needed. There are lizards, snails, scorpions, whatever. And don't complain about the A.C. There isn't any. If there is, it's *guasto*—broken.

This year we arrived with two other couples and from the moment we stepped out of our rented cars we knew the whole thing was a mistake. The dirt road that led from the main drive to the villa was far too long and perilously bumpy. By the time we reached the villa after hobbling in the worst way for almost a mile, the picturesque landscape, with its olive trees, vineyards, and a large pig farm we had spotted along the way, had lost their charm. All we wanted was to get to our rooms, take off our clothes, and hop into the pool. But when we arrived early that Saturday afternoon, the help was still busy cleaning the house after the previous guests had left the day before.

Though gracious, the woman mopping the floor was visibly peeved, while her husband, wrench in hand after sweating over the plumbing in the kitchen in his yellowed wife-beater, was no less irked by our presence. Quietly, we left all our stuff in the car and walked around to inspect the grounds. Our villa, as we discovered, was not isolated but abutted another villa a few yards away, and another on the other side of that one,

forming a sort of U-shaped atrium in the middle of which sat
a raised swimming pool. My heart sank. Might as well have
an inflatable pool for toddlers, I thought. What I'd longed
for was one of those long, sunken-in-the-ground infinity
pools where you float serenely on quiet afternoons and with
one breaststroke think you're about to reach for the soul of
Italy, the genius of the Renaissance, and the very essence of
antiquity. Just float and heed the turtledoves cooing above
ground on this clearest sky man ever saw on planet Earth and
you got your glimpse of eternity.

The house was typically *agroturismo*—a tastefully
converted ancient peasant stone house that rents for around
$10,000 a week during peak summer months. The realtor's
catalogue, like all catalogues, did not misrepresent nor
distort; it simply fanned your fantasies and airbrushed the
rest. The big picture spelled Chianti of your dreams; the devil
was in the details.

We had arrived after a week in Rome as we'd done every
year. Sweaty, exhausted, lugging lots of dirty laundry, we
expected to do what we'd done every other year: throw
everything in the washing machine then hop into the pool.
Instead the matronly owner of the property who lived in one
of the adjacent houses informed us that her live-in Polynesian
maid would gladly do our laundry on Monday at a reasonable
rate. When we asked, her reasonable rate plus the added
charge for folding boggled the mind. Thank you very much,
but we'd do our laundry in town. Inconvenient, but doable,
since we'd spotted a *lavanderia* on our way to the house. 'As
you wish,' she said.

When my wife knocked at her door later that evening and asked for the WiFi code she was told that there was no internet. Besides, said the old lady, we were here to relax not to send emails back and forth. If we wanted DVDs, however, she'd be happy to let us borrow them at a reasonable rate. When my wife protested and said that the brochure had advertised free WiFi, the landlady explained that this was a mistake. 'Besides, you are here to relax,' she insisted.

We began to feel trapped in one of those horror movies where tourists are subjected to all manner of insidious agonies and tricks, driven out of their minds, and finally picked off one by one. We had already paid for the house and given a deposit. Our hands were tied. My wife's advice, when she came back, was simply to enjoy an evening swim, have drinks on the veranda, and then have a pasta dinner with all manner of veggies and salad and gelato under the trees.

By night all hell broke loose. As none of the windows had screens nor the beds any nets, and since no one had thought of shutting the bedroom windows on this hottest summer in Europe's history, we awoke to find our bodies littered with mosquito bites beyond anything resembling an infestation of bedbugs. But that wasn't the worst of it. What truly terrified me that night was a sudden, piercing shriek just above my head that made me think that a piglet on the farm was being butchered on our bed. It proved to be, once I turned on the lights, a panic-stricken bat circling madly about the room until I chased it away with a large towel.

'All you had to do was light a citronella candle and place it on the window ledge. It stays lit through the night and repels all insects,' said the landlady when we complained the next morning. What about the *zanzariera*, I asked, referring to the mosquito net. The *zanzariera* was in the closet. As was the citronella. 'All you had to do was ask. We're not savages, you know,' muttered the splenetic old lady as she shuffled away on her aching knees. She'd seen the likes of us for ages and had no patience.

To make matters worse one of the couples was on the verge of divorcing and was constantly heard sparring and bickering—politely, but in perpetual whispers as they hissed at each to each, while their pouting twins were constantly texting to their friends in New Jersey. The other couple was no better. They had what they were persuaded was a six-year-old genius girl who was already being taught a child's version of *The Divine Comedy*. 'Tomorrow we're doing Michelangelo,' the father said on our second night there. And on Wednesday *La Traviata,* I jeered. 'Aren't your boys interested in Italian culture?' asked the father in front of my sons, who were just coming out of the pool.

'Not in the slightest,' replied one of them.

'Why so?'

'Because we wade in ignorance,' retorted my eldest, who couldn't stand either the father or the daughter or the soft-spoken mother.

Two things put the finishing blow. Early on Monday morning we awoke not only with mosquito bites all over our bodies again—despite the citronella—but to the loud snarls of a tractor chortling away at precisely 8am When we left to visit one of the wine villages nearby, the tractor was still chuffing away and giving vigorous belches. When I finally mustered the courage to knock at the landlady's door to complain that the woken all of us up, she said there was nothing she could do. 'This is a farm, you know. Not everyone is a tourist here.' 'But couldn't they start an hour later?' I asked. 'They have to eat, poor people, don't they? Olives, wine, and pigs, they don't just happen, you know.'

'We've been had,' we said that night over our usual fare of spaghetti, tomatoes, salad and gelato.

The next morning, same thing: impossible to sleep past eight. Expecting to hear one of the farmers gun the engine gave our morning sleep a restless quality. To say nothing of the loutish farmers hollering at each other, when all they were doing was having a friendly little chat.

The coup de grâce came on Wednesday. We had been to visit Montalcino, about an hour and a half away, because the father of the genius girl was very keen on buying a case of Brunello wines and having it shipped to the States. It was a very hot afternoon and, eager to get back and rest, the father of the twins had accelerated the engine as he forded the long dirt road leading to the house. Because of the bumpy road, the gas tank of his rented Mercedes happened to scrape a boulder he hadn't spotted. He stopped the car, as we all did behind him, and could easily observe a large gash leaking gas. We called the house and asked the landlady to call the car rental service. 'Why did you need to speed?' she asked.

Which is when the father of the twins let the old lady have it: *we should have been told about this dangerously long stretch.* The bickering wife started yelling as well: *why were we misled into thinking this was a secluded house.* Not to be outdone, I too lost it with her and gave her a piece of my mind. We were going to report her to the tourism agency, we were going to ask for our money back, we were going to blacken her name and her property on the web. And by the way, this is not even a pool. *E una secchia, è una vasca, è una vergogna,* I yelled in Italian. This isn't a pool, it's a bucket, it's a tub, it's a shame.

We were a tinderbox. What blew the fuse was calling the car rental agency. They would arrive the next day. When I asked at what time, the agent said he didn't know. So basically some of us were going to be prisoners in the house. We were already prisoners, said another. 'So now you'll have to relax,' said the matron. 'We can no longer relax. You've made sure of that.'

By the end of that day, we were no longer on speaking terms with her.

On the morning of our fifth day, the old lady had one of her farmhands bring us a large bottle of virgin olive oil and a small basket of tomatoes. When I made to tip him, he refused and sped away. We examined the bottle, sprinkled her oil over salt and the sliced tomatoes and were, almost against our will, suddenly in heaven. That same evening, after the rental agency replaced the car, two bottles of wine mysteriously appeared on our doorsteps. Though we drank the wine reluctantly and with resentment in our hearts, there was no denying it: this was superb. On my way out in the morning, I crossed the old lady and shouted a breezy remark that was meant to sound more offhand than genuine. 'The wine was very good last night.'

'Yes, it is fantastic?' she said. But seeing I wasn't about to make further concessions, she answered her own question: *Of course it's fantastic. It's the best in the region,* she grumbled. When we came back from visiting Volpaia, my favorite small town, three bottles were standing on our doorstep. Plus a huge basket of the most luscious figs we'd ever seen. And another basket of tomatoes. This is penance big-time, one of us said. But there we were, all twelve of us, sitting at a huge table under the trees, drinking her wine, eating a huge meal of pasta, with fresh tomatoes and the most redolent basil picked from her garden. This is the most beautiful place on earth. Even the swimming pool had become beautiful, and one day, I told everyone, we'll even miss the damned tractor every morning and the belching pigs.

The next morning we greeted her warmly. Wearing a butcher's leather apron, the old lady looked hunched and humbled and sad. Suddenly I felt as though we had offended her and she was repaying our makeshift gratitude with genuine kindness and understanding. 'Tonight I have a surprise for you.'

'What surprise?' I asked, fearing the worst.

Vedrete, you'll see. And off she shoveled on her grieving bunions.

Late in the afternoon, on our last day, on parking our cars after visiting Assisi, we spotted two handymen at our doorstep carrying two large, wrapped packages. 'The *signora* wanted to give you this. They are the best cuts. She hopes you had a pleasant stay.' I unfolded the mysterious paper wrapping and saw meat. What is it, I gestured. 'It's the *maiale,*' he explained, the pig.

'Which pig?'

'The *signora* had it butchered this morning for your dinner tonight.'

When I looked again I saw that there was enough meat for a battalion. After a hasty swim, everyone got busy. My boys washed the salad, the twin girls put aside their cell phones and sliced the tomatoes, someone started boiling the large vat of water for our usual spaghetti, while the adults worked the grill outside. We picked oregano from the garden and the rosemary from one of the many bushes outside the doorstep and sprinkled it on the meat. Once the steaks were set on the grill a wonderful aroma began to permeate the air. Someone said that the meat should be juicy, not dry. Genius girl set the table for twelve, one of my boys lit the citronella on the table, and then the father who had bought a case of Brunello had a brainstorm and decided that life was only lived once and that at least one of his precious Brunellos needed to be opened tonight. No one objected, and right away we began comparing his Brunello to the signora's artisanal wine. There was no comparison. The Brunello was sublime. But the homemade wine wasn't bad either. And then one by one we sat at the table, feeling that this indeed was a feast and that if we had to do it all over again, there was no doubt that we would. Including the gash in the car? Including the gash in the car. Including the mosquitoes and the tractor and the poor bat that fluttered like crazy in the middle of the night? Including bats and insects. Including the *signora*? Most certainly the *signora*. We were learning to do something we should have done from the very first minute we'd arrived. Enjoy ourselves, enjoy one another, and, in the words of the old *signora*, learn to relax.

FUCHSIA DUNLOP is a British cook and writer specialising in Chinese cuisine. She has written four books, including the award-winning *Shark's Fin and Sichuan Pepper: A Sweet-Sour Memoir of Eating in China*. Her work has appeared in numerous publications and she won James Beard awards in 2012 and 2013.

CHASING THE TAIL OF CHIUCHOW

Fuchsia Dunlop

I t was noon in Shantou, the southern Chinese river
port also known as Swatow. A party of chefs and food
writers had gathered around the table, and lunch was
about to begin. The waitresses started bringing platters
of food from the kitchens: stewed goose with all its
accoutrements, cold fish with yellow bean sauce, and
tiny fried shrimp. As each beautiful dish emerged, it
was greeted with a round of lusty noises of appreciation:
Pwooargh! Ooooagh! Phfooagh! After nearly two decades
of eating my way around China, I'd never heard anything
like the raucous joy with which these Chiuchow gourmets
expressed their approval of our lunch.

   Cantonese cuisine is supposedly the best known of all
China's regional cuisines. It was Cantonese immigrants who
flocked to the American West in the nineteenth-century

gold rush, bringing with them their own ingredients and setting up the first Chinese restaurants in the country. Even today, most Chinese restaurants in the West offer dishes that are, broadly speaking, Cantonese, such as sweet and sour pork and lacquered roast duck. But perhaps because Cantonese cuisine seems so familiar, its true sophistication and diversity are rarely appreciated. And for evidence of the complexity of Cantonese cuisine, one need look no further than the Chiuchow, or Chaozhou, cooking region in Guangdong province.

This tiny pocket of northeastern Guangdong, named in English after its ancient capital Chaozhou but these days dominated by the modern metropolis of Shantou, is home to one of China's most thrilling little regional cuisines. There are hotbeds of Chiuchow cooking in Hong Kong and Thailand, where immigrants from the region have settled, but if you live in Europe or America the chances are you've never heard of it. The only named Chiuchow delicacy that pops up with any regularity on mainstream Chinese menus in the West is the *chao zhou fen guo*, a translucent steamed dumpling stuffed with a mix of finely chopped pork, vegetables and peanuts. If you're really lucky, you might come across some aromatic stewed duck made in the Chiuchow goose style, but in my experience, it's a rarity.

I'd been chasing the tail of Chiuchow cooking ever since my first encounter with it in a small, cramped upstairs dining room in the Hong Kong district of Sheung Wan. There, thanks to my friend Rose, who brought me to the restaurant with some friends, I had my first taste of the region's shellfish

congees, raw marinated crabs, and strips of taro frosted
with silvery sugar. From that moment on, I sought out
Chiuchow food whenever I was in Hong Kong, mostly in the
Chiuchow enclave of Kowloon City, where shopkeepers chop
their braised goose on wooden boards and the Chong Fat
restaurant cooks up scrumptious regional delicacies. I longed
to travel to the Chiuchow region itself, but it wasn't until
many years later that I finally made it there.

'Ma ma ma ma ma ma ma ma,' said Xu Jun, trying to teach
me the eight different tones of Shantou dialect. They all
sounded similar to me, even though I'm a Mandarin speaker.
But then the dialect of Shantou, the modern capital of the
Chiuchow region, is notorious in China, where they say
only native speakers can grasp its subtle modulations. ('The
most difficult language in the world to learn,' one taxi driver
assured me.) The proliferation of regional tongues is one of
the great frustrations for a foreigner learning Chinese. You
can slave away at your Mandarin, and develop a passing
acquaintance with a few local dialects, but as soon as you visit
a new part of the country, you won't be able to understand
a word people say when they talk amongst themselves.
When it comes to food, however, this extraordinary regional
diversity is a blessing, because the closer you look at so-called
'Chinese cuisine', the more it expands and proliferates, like a
computer-generated fractal pattern.

Xu Jun, Zheng Yuhui and their friends took me in hand as
soon as I arrived in Shantou, a grey metropolis in one of the

industrial heartlands of southern China. Within a couple of hours, they had whisked me off to the home of a famous local food writer, Zhang Xinmin; to a market where we surveyed radiantly fresh fish and intriguing dim sum; and to the home of the secretary of the local gourmet association, who was putting the finishing touches to his precise mise-en-place for that evening's gastronomic adventures. A large potful of pork, cuttlefish and Yunnan ham simmered away on a slow flame on his stove, perfuming the entire apartment. As we inhaled its gorgeous aromas, Zheng Yuhui showed me photographs of dishes he and Zhang had prepared for their dinner parties. From what I could make out, they spent most of their free time cooking in Zhang's smartly appointed kitchen, amazing their friends with magnificent dishes and then posting the pictures to their *weibo* accounts, the Chinese equivalent of Twitter, where they each have legions of followers.

In that huge private room at the Jianye restaurant, they gave me my first real initiation into Shantou cooking. I'd had the famous aromatic stewed goose in Hong Kong, but never with all its trimmings. Here, there was not only goose flesh, succulent and lightly spiced, with a garlic and vinegar dip; also, on separate plates were arranged creamy goose liver, crisp intestines, jellied blood, crunchy gizzards, wings, feet and heads, each laid on a bed of tender beancurd and drizzled with some of the bird's delicious cooking juices. Later, we tried some of the seafood for which the region is also renowned, prepared with a minimalism I was told was typical of the local culinary style.

'We really emphasise harmony between nature and man,' said Zhang Xinmin. 'We make stringent demands of our ingredients because, even by general Cantonese standards, our seasoning is so light. You see these crabs,' he said, gesturing at a pair of the opened crustaceans, resplendent with orange roe, spread out with their claws and legs on a platter. 'They are steamed with no seasonings at all. In Sichuanese cuisine, you have many flavours used in combination; here, it's all about *yuan zhi yuan wei*, the original taste of ingredients, with seasonings often added afterwards, as a separate dip.'

Sure enough, the crabs came with dipping dishes of garlicky vinegar, and the cold steamed fish with a punchy, fermented bean sauce from the town of Puning. Later, we shared an oyster omelette served with fish sauce speckled with pepper, and deep-fried shrimp balls with a tangerine syrup. 'In the Qing Dynasty,' said Zhang, 'this region produced most of China's sugar, which is why you'll find a certain sweetness in our food.'

While foreigners don't even recognise Chiuchow as a separate cooking region, Shantou gourmets are fiercely insistent on the distinction between their own lively culinary culture and that of the ancient regional capital, Chaozhou. 'Shantou people see Chaozhou as backward and bumpkinish,' Zheng Yuhui told me. 'So if you ask a Shantou person if they're from Chaozhou, they may be offended. Moreover, you'll always taste the finest food in Shantou.' Zheng vehemently rejects the term 'Chiuchow cuisine', preferring to speak instead of 'Shantou' or 'Chaoshan' (Chaozhou and Shantou) cuisine.

After lunch, I persuaded Zheng and his friends to take me on a tour of the old part of the city, a relic of its status as a treaty port imposed on China by the Western powers after the nineteenth-century Opium Wars. Nothing could have prepared me for this glimpse of the lost world of Shantou's foreign concession, which was like a ghostly shadow of the old French quarter of Shanghai. One or two buildings, like the English post office, had been restored and were still in use; the rest, street after street, block after block of early twentieth-century tenements, had been left to crumble into the polluted air. Shrubs sprouted from roofs and ledges; weeds had insinuated themselves between bricks and mortar. A few residents had clung on, their brightly coloured washing strung out on the shattered balconies, but most of the buildings were deserted. The whole quarter, I was told, was slated for demolition.

Before I left Shantou, Zheng took me for a breakfast crawl of the backstreets, seeking out some of his favourite snack shops. In London and Hong Kong I was used to the dim sum version of *cheung fun*, those slithery sheets of rice paste embracing plump prawns, deep-fried doughsticks or barbecued pork. Here, in a thriving breakfast café, cooks spread the thin layers of liquidised rice with broken eggs, minced pork, leafy greens, tiny oysters and prawns, steamed them swiftly and then roughly folded them. They served the pasta with a soy sauce dressing and steaming bowls of pork offal soup. In another café, we ate a soup of rice noodles and beef balls. The lean beef had been beaten by hand with metal cudgels, whipped up into a taut, springy state so the cooked meatballs were actually crunchy in the mouth.

Despite the withering scorn with which Shantou locals viewed the old city of Chaozhou, as a foreign visitor I found it irresistible. Although the city is now surrounded by ceramics factories, the historic part of town has the kind of sleepy charm that has been erased in many parts of China by reckless modernisation. Under the colonnades of the restored Memorial Arch Street I found long-established snack shops and bakeries that pandered to the notoriously sweet tooth of the Chiuchownese. In the Hurongquan café I tried the house speciality, 'Duck egg twists', glutinous riceballs stuffed with bean paste and served in a sweetened broth with chunks of sweet potato, gingko nuts, silver ear fungus and the white grains known as Job's tears.

Nearby, a bakery was turning out golden pastries impressed with patterns from their wooden moulds, and stuffed with a scintillating sweet pork flavoured with fermented tofu and garlic. Legend has it that this sweetmeat was born out of a labour dispute in the late Qing Dynasty. A disgruntled baker, so they say, stormed out of his job after an attempted act of sabotage, having mixed all the ingredients in the storeroom together: fatty pork, peanuts, sesame seeds, garlic, syrup, flour, fermented tofu and wine. The boss's wife noticed that the mess had a captivating aroma, so she used it as a stuffing in the next day's cakes, which were received by their customers with rapturous approval.

In one of the backstreets, I came across a few old ladies sorting tea-leaves with their hands on bamboo trays, and countless tea vendors. Chaozhou is the original home of *gong fu cha*, a tea-drinking practice that has become fashionable all over China. Roasted Iron Buddha teas are brewed in miniature pots, and the caramel-coloured infusion poured into tiny bowls. The bittersweet liquid is as sharpening as an espresso coffee. In the Chiuchow region, it is served before and after meals, and at any time of day. In the slow streets of the old city, shopkeepers sit all day on wooden chairs outside their establishments, their tea gear arranged on china trays, sipping tea, smoking cigarettes and chatting.

Every morning, one lane in the southern part of the old town was thronged with market shoppers. Goose vendors stood before glass cabinets hung with their glossy birds, still warm from the pot, ready to chop them to order. A couple of sellers offered cooked, cooled fish arrayed in bamboo baskets. There were freshly made snacks: fluffy heart-shaped rice cakes stained green by mulberry leaves, rice-paste dim sum stuffed with fragrant chives, and little cups of steamed translucent dim sum stuffed with minced pork that had been fried with a salty pickle. A woman stuffed raw minced pork into pockets of tofu and sections of hollow bitter melons that customers could take home and cook for their dinner.

Even for a well-travelled Chinese foodhound like me, Chaozhou was full of surprises. Most amazing was the urban goatherd I met on a busy thoroughfare near my hotel. His four white goats stood, tethered, on a wooden cart on the back of his bicycle, looking curiously around at the traffic and the neon signs, their udders bulging. He milked them as they stood there, bagging up the milk and selling it to passing customers. 'Just boil it and it's good to drink,' he told me.

By the end of my visit, I was beginning to have a richer
sense of the Chiuchow style: of its cold, cooked fish with
their pungent dips, fresh steamed seafood, rich congees, rice
noodles, cakes and sweetmeats. From the outside, it might
seem to be collapsed into a generic Cantonese style. From the
inside, it was a vibrant culinary region with a proud sense
of its own identity. Chaozhou, and Shantou too, were places
to throw out all one's preconceptions about Chinese food,
and open one's eyes to the seemingly infinite variety of the
country's regional cuisines.

MARCUS SAMUELSSON is a five-time James Beard award-winning chef and author. He is the owner of Red Rooster Harlem, the co-founder of Three Goats Organization, and the co-creator of Food Republic, the online community for men who want to learn to eat and drink well, and live smart.

FACE TO FACE WITH FUGU

Marcus Samuelsson

The story was always the same with these young cooks. After fifteen-hour shifts chopping and peeling, sautéing and braising, we were always looking for ways to blow off steam. I've cooked in France, Switzerland, Sweden, and on cruise ships, but the need to turn down the intensity after you left the kitchen didn't need any translation. We wanted to have fun.

When I was first starting out, beers with the guys meant looking for girls and showing off our battle wounds from hot pans and sharp knives. But after a few years of working hard and partying hard, I started to get an itch for something stronger. I wanted to taste the world outside of the same sauces I was making day in, day out. Everyone insisted the best food was French food (and I wasn't about to argue this point with my chefs at Georges Blanc), but I also knew there were flavors I hadn't experienced yet. The late nights out with the other chefs became fewer and fewer. I was saving money to travel to Japan and eat fugu—a potentially deadly puffer fish that could kill you if it wasn't prepared the right way.

I had first heard about fugu from my high school sweetheart's family. Christina's father was Swedish but her mother was Japanese, and dinnertime at their house was a virtual passport into a whole other culture. While my own mother might have opened a can of peaches and drizzled the syrup over some whipped cream (a delicious, if not safe, treat as she wasn't the best cook), snacks at Christina's meant dried and seasoned cuttlefish or cold cucumber salad tossed in white miso and topped with bonito flakes.

These were flavors I wasn't used to—fish at the Samuelsson house was usually smoked, cured or folded into mashed potatoes. Sure, we had access to the freshest fish (some of my best childhood memories were fishing with my father and Uncle Torsten in Smögen), but having it sliced raw and presented with nothing more than a drop of soy sauce and a dab of wasabi forever changed me. And there was a fish that could actually kill someone? I knew I had to discover this creature for myself.

By that time I was twenty-one and working as a junior chef at the Victoria-Jungfrau Interlaken resort in Switzerland. While my friends were saving money for cars and other spoils, I didn't have enough money to take a girl out. I wanted to pinch every penny and save every bill for the trip to Tokyo that would invariably change my perspective. My focus was razor sharp and I even picked up extra shifts to get to my goal faster. Here was a challenge that pitted man against a potentially slow and painful death brought on by an improperly prepared dish. My head couldn't be clearer.

Curiosity doesn't have a number to it. As a cook you're rich and poor. Your palate is rich but getting to experience all the flavors in the world can cost you. In this case, I had two things that I needed to precisely plan—saving enough money to get me to Tokyo and scheduling the time when I would go. Fugu is only available October through January so I had to make sure everything lined up perfectly. Luckily, Christina had family in Japan who could host me, so all I needed to do was pack a few clothes, running shoes, a notebook, and enough money to keep me in Japan for ten days and a meal of blowfish.

Here was this place that was all about the other—a new culture, a language I couldn't understand, and a dish whose safety was in the hands of another chef. If it's not prepared properly to remove its toxins, one lick of the wrong part and you're a goner. But I didn't even have the bandwidth to think about all the odds against me. Even though it felt like I was the only black person in this homogeneous country, I was like a kid in a cultural candy store. I remember walking into the basement of the famed department store Takashimaya and experiencing what a real Japanese tea ceremony was about. Three hours of sitting on your knees makes a bikram yoga session look easy. I walked around the basements of department stores for hours, taking in all the colors and smells of the bento boxes and rice cakes that were put on display. Trips to Tsujiki, Tokyo's (if not the world's) most notable fish market, meant sushi for breakfast, and I ate more ramen that week than I have in the past two years. (And I really love ramen.)

To keep me busy and help me curb my spending before the big meal, I was allowed to observe chefs in a sushi restaurant. Mind you, I say observed, not worked with. These were strictly 'Look, Don't Touch' hours and I was instructed to stand silently in the corner while these small men with big voices shaped hundreds and hundreds of perfectly crafted bites of sushi.

In the middle of my trip, Christina's aunt walked me over to a fugu restaurant in Setagaya. I remember thinking we were in the wrong place because here I was standing in front of a nondescript office building, this woman pointing down to below the ground. I ventured down to the sub-sub-basement of this building and into the foyer of a fugu restaurant. Since these specialty spots are only open the three months out of the year you can get the fish, one might wonder what the chefs do for work the other nine months. But with the kind of precision, skill and craft they have to have to handle fugu, who cared? All I knew was that I had made it here.

Forget about asking for a menu; here fugu is the star and they will let you know how you should eat it. First, they bring out the whole fish to show you. If you've ever seen what puffer fish looks like, it's a speckled creature with two large beady eyes on the sides of its head. The spiked exterior is used as a defense mechanism and, when threatened, they can fill up their extremely elastic bellies full of water, immediately stabbing their predator. The puffer that was brought to my table knew what was about to happen, its clear and perfect eyesight bore right into my psyche.

It was the first and last time I hesitated during that meal. After twenty years I can't remember the name of the restaurant, but I remember those seven courses. First up was sashimi, delicate and almost sweet, followed by pieces fried in a super-light tempura batter that didn't feel greasy. Next up, a piece of poached fish. The main course was a rustic, almost soupy, dish, composed of rice and dashi, that wonderfully simple yet complex-tasting Japanese broth, which was made with the fugu bones. I didn't have two nickels to rub together when I was done, but it was so worth it. That meal was close to perfection for me.

It also really messed me up.

You know the moment when you realize you've been missing the party? I was there and I did something that took me on a different path; once you see something great, you're even further away from it. How did they do this? These guys weren't French, they weren't Michelin-starred and they didn't wear tall chef hats. I was a young black chef and I was taught the best food came from France. This meal threw a big wrench into what I knew up to that point and my future didn't seem so planned out for me. Guess what? That made it better.

Nowadays you can see almost every corner of this earth on Google maps, and even learn how to fillet a fugu on YouTube. Advancements in travel and technology give us access to things our parents never dreamed about. With so many new and even newer versions coming out so fast, we often gripe if authenticity gets lost in translation. But it's not about mourning how things used to be done—you have to go and experience these things for yourself, whether it's finding ways to preserve a tradition or thinking of different flavors that will make a dish your own.

Through all my travels around the world, one thing has always stayed true: I don't eat. I taste. And this ever-long journey of taste hits me the same way whether I'm at a *nasi goreng* stand in Singapore, eating warm beef tartare in Ethiopia, chowing down on a fish sandwich on the beach in Barbados, or eating a fugu dinner. It's my curiosity about different cultures that keeps me tasting and seeking, and I don't ever want to lose my constant search for the next bite that I have to have.

DANIEL VAUGHN is the barbecue editor for *Texas Monthly* magazine and the author of *The Prophets of Smoked Meat: A Journey Through Texas Barbecue*. He is a trained architect living in Dallas, Texas, with two young children and his beautiful wife Jennifer.

HIGH ON THE HOG IN GEORGIA

Daniel Vaughn

Warner Robins, Georgia, or Wichita Falls, Texas? My boss gave me the choice between two air force bases with equally dull renovation projects to oversee and, like most of the travel choices at that point in my life, barbecue was the tie-breaker. Georgia's foreign soil seemed full of possibilities. I was still working as an architect, but I could feel my design career winding down with every passing month. I was in the midst of writing a book on barbecue during my free nights and weekends. Everyone warned me about quitting a very good job for the prospect of steady book sales. Regardless, my mind couldn't help but wander toward dreams of making my living from my passion: barbecue. In the meantime, company-funded expeditions in search of foreign barbecue traditions were a welcome diversion. Traveling across my home state of Texas and writing about its rich barbecue culture had become second nature over the last several years, but my only Georgia barbecue guidebook was *Atlanta magazine*'s 'BBQ 2010'. In the opening article Jim Auchmutey wrote that 'Atlanta and Georgia are chameleons of "'cue". He contended that the only barbecue constant around the state was Brunswick stew. The Georgia style was going to be hard to pin down, but my job would take me there monthly and barbecue would be a constant on the itinerary.

April: With so many other options, the only pork that ended up on my plate at Fox Bros. Bar-B-Q was a few deep-fried ribs. Jonathan and Justin Fox hail from Fort Worth and opened this namesake joint in 2007 after they couldn't find brisket to their liking in town. How very Texan. Thick slices of smoked brisket arrived, some from the lean end and a few from the fatty point end. All of it had an overt smokiness from the blackened crust surrounding each slice. The fat clinging to the 'lean' slices was adequately smoked to need no trimming, and the slices from the point were laced with wonderful fat that just required the additional heat from my tongue to hit its melting point. This was comfort food for a Texan, so it was surely some of Georgia's best. Side items, I would come to discover, are anything but an afterthought in Atlanta. The soul food traditions inform the menu offerings in ways that go from comforting to irreverent. Take the Fox-a-roni—a creamy mix of large pasta shells and cheese is dunked into a bowl of traditional Brunswick stew. Mix and enjoy.

May: Could lightning strike twice at Fox Bros.? Texas style spare ribs beckoned from the specials board. The ends of each rib were snarls of melted fat and smoky pork with a pleasant chewiness. Picking at the pockets of pork between bones and tendons is like a meaty scavenger hunt that can continue as long as you're willing. Bathing in the familiarity I moved from rib to rib, but I would spread my wings on the next visit to Georgia.

June: If Fox Bros. was on the familiar Texas end of the barbecue spectrum, this tiny renovated liquor store stretched all the way to the other end, somewhere in South Korea, where Heirloom Market chef Jiyeon Lee was born and gained fame as a Korean pop star (seriously). She met Cody Taylor in Atlanta and they opened this joint, where you're as likely to find tempura-fried sweet potato slices—which are stunning— as you are Southern pulled pork.

I was now traveling with my client who was a military man with little knowledge of my barbecue prowess. I needed this place to be impressive for a couple of reasons. I knew I'd be traveling with him for the foreseeable future, so a good meal meant he might defer to me for our monthly dining options (more barbecue, please!). We'd also be driving for two hours after our meal to reach Warner Robins. I didn't want it to feel any longer than it had to.

The Korean fried chicken was sold out. Able stand-ins were stewed collard greens wrapped in a rich broth that had bite, and the Brunswick stew with corn kernels, large chunks of tomatoes and a hearty amount of barely shredded meat all held together loosely by a thinnish brick-red broth. Worcestershire and sugar stood out too, and the ingredients hadn't yet broken down into the more familiar smooth texture. It looked like what a trained culinary professional may have arrived at when asked to make a 'stew'. It had all of the classic elements along with a freedom unstifled by an old Georgia family recipe.

A simple slice of brisket was stunningly well smoked (getting the lean slices to proper doneness while keeping them moist is an art), and, quickly downing half of a very atypical pork sandwich that was too well executed to call a gimmick, I was ready to declare Heirloom Market the future of Southern barbecue. The spicy chili-coated cubes of smoked pork coupled with the crunchy acidity of the kimchee coleslaw tassel on top was a happy marriage of two traditions within a well-made potato bun. Atlanta may have been home to legitimate barbecue joints since the early twentieth century, but the fact that a specific style never took hold of the city has provided it a distinct opportunity for culinary innovation that is not obliged to the yoke of traditionalism. Rise up, Atlanta.

Martin's BBQ is literally across the street from the jobsite at Robins Air Force Base. Keeping a strong grasp on my notion that good brisket is hard to find outside of Texas (I can be hard-headed, even with the very positive experiences the month and day immediately preceding) I stuck with pork. The ribs were fair while the pulled pork was chopped earlier in the day and had dried out somewhat. It needed the moisture of the vinegar sauce. I plodded through the meal, content in my assumptions, but curious about the promising slices of brisket in the paper-lined baskets across the table from me. With a full mouth, an extended fork and an inquisitive look from me, I gained a permissive grunt from my generous client. I took a slice. The beef was moist, tender and had a deep smokiness—serious brisket. Outside I found their gas-fired Southern Pride smoker. I'm more of a fan of meat cooked only with wood, but tipped my hat to the pitmaster, who provided superior smoked beef from what I consider inferior equipment.

July: After a mid-afternoon flight, my client and I were to meet Bill Addison, who had authored that Atlanta BBQ 2010 list. Texas thunderstorms had other ideas. Bill was on deadline and his procrastination wouldn't allow for a late meal, so we were on our own. The previous month's meals worked out well enough that my client left our choice up to me. To understand the barbecue scene I needed somewhere that offered respectable food whose popularity might outweigh its quality. Bill's answer was Fat Matt's Rib Shack. If you're a movie buff then this joint might sound familiar. When asked for a rib joint recommendation in Atlanta, George Clooney's character in *Up in the Air* responds without hesitation, 'Fat Matt's. Bring a bib.'

The smells wafting through the air brought back a childhood familiarity that I had almost forgotten. When I was growing up in Ohio we went to church with a woman named Carol. Her husband Jerry never joined her at church, but was instead known for his barbecued chicken and his drinking problem. He would sit for hours beside his charcoal grill with a can of beer in one hand, a jug full of sweet barbecue sauce in the other, just basting away while the entire neighborhood was covered with the smell of grilling, or more specifically the smell of burning sugar from the basting sauce. This was the smell of Fat Matt's patio.

Anthony Bourdain put down a rack of Fat Matt's ribs on his show *The Layover*. I go by @BBQsnob on Twitter so it seemed like a personal message when he opened his meal there with the line, 'Okay, barbecue snobs and food nerds, I know it's not real barbecue.' What he means is that they pre-cook their ribs and grill them over direct heat. They do not smoke meat, nor do they pretend to. Brisket is not on the menu nor will you find tempura-battered anything. When you ask for sauce on the side they assume you just want more sauce, not unadulterated meat. How would it smell like the burnt sugar of a backyard cookout any other way? We got a little of everything, which included a chopped pork sandwich more akin to a sloppy joe, Brunswick stew that had simmered beyond the point where any single ingredient could be recognized, and a rack of ribs whose meat was literally dropping off the bones from being so tender. The charred flavor from the fire was secondary only to the vinegar-heavy tomato sauce. Juicy breast meat beneath crispy chicken skin didn't have even a whiff of smoke, but it was grilled with such a deft hand that I had to peek back inside on my way out just to make sure Jerry wasn't back there with a beer manning the grill.

August: I travelled alone on this trip. The weather held up and Bill Addison was able to meet me at Community Q, where I drove immediately after securing my rental car. Dave Roberts opened this place in 2009 after working with two Atlanta-area barbecue legends—Dave Poe and Sam

Huff. We'll get to them in a few months. The menu here was the widest I'd found in Georgia. Not only did they have pork, ribs, brisket and chicken, but they also had beef short ribs, which are fatty bricks of roast-like beef perched atop what could be mistaken for a human femur. They are big and they are very hard to cook well. Although Bill had me prepared to love the brisket and pork ribs, we agreed that the smoky beef rib, with its pull-apart tenderness and aggressive black pepper seasoning, won the day.

I would be remiss not to mention the 'Mac N Cheese'. It's not often in Georgia that a specific side item gets as much attention as Brunswick stew does, but in Atlanta it's all about rigatoni with plenty of cheddar, Monterey Jack and parmesan, all mixed in with a hefty amount of cream. The recipe's provenance is debated, no matter the recipe's origination you can find it at Community Q, Dave Poe's BBQ, Sam's BBQ1 and Grand Champion BBQ.

Being unhindered by time and wanting to prolong my temporary escape from real work, we left Community Q bound for the brand new Bone Lick BBQ. Mike LaSage had been doing a weekly barbecue menu within P'cheen restaurant and he called it Bone Lick BBQ. Atlanta magazine offered high praise to this tiny joint within a restaurant in their BBQ 2010 article, so Bill was anxious to try it now that it had its own space and a daily menu of smoked meat. I hate to carp too heavily on a place that just opened, but it's also hard to quiet my inner critic. Based on one visit they were experiencing some considerable growing pains.

September: A crisis on the jobsite brought me straight to Warner Robins, where I arrived just in time for lunch at Martin's BBQ. I ate more great brisket and opted this time for some well-smoked turkey breast. Fresh-cut French fries and hand-battered okra rounded out what was once again a great meal. Then I did it again the next day, and the sausage isn't bad either.

October: Those hot Georgia summers were giving way to beautiful fall skies, and the architecture was starting to get in the way of the barbecue hunts. I had just returned from a weekend with the Southern Foodways Alliance that had altered my perspective on my place in the food writing world. It was the SFA symposium of food thinkers, writers, purveyors and cooks. My fellow attendees cared about the barbecue book I had nearly completed and encouraged me to take the leap. At the beginning of the symposium I introduced myself as an architect. By the second day it felt more natural to say I was an author. I was among peers.

Back at the jobsite a morning meeting mercifully ended early. I left the group who went to Martin's again and I drove north to Jackson, the home of Fresh Air Bar-B-Q since 1929. It felt good to be on the back roads with nothing but time and an appetite. I was seeking a therapeutic mental refuge in barbecue as much I was seeking smoked meat.

I had to laugh, as I walked to the door through the gravel parking lot, that the only thing tainting the crisp blue sky was a plume from the smokestack of a nearby power plant. I guess it was all fresh air out here in 1929, but no longer. I enjoyed the brevity of the menu: you could get a plate of gently sauced pork with slaw and Brunswick stew, or you could get a larger plate. I thought this must be the Georgia Style that Robert F. Moss discussed in his book *Barbecue: The History of an American Institution*, where he describes a dry-ish chopped pork lightly doused with a thin, red vinegar sauce along with a side of Brunswick stew. Smoking only hams made for a drier meat but the finely chopped pork hadn't verged into sawdust territory. A hearty Brunswick stew contained a bit of what looked like ground beef along with potatoes and corn. The bright green slaw was finely chopped with just enough mayonnaise dressing to hold it together. This was pork meant for piling onto bread and topping with that slaw, and that's just how I polished it off.

Just up the road was The Blind Pig, where I was soon seated with a tray of ribs, beans, stew and an exemplary pulled pork sandwich. Pork shoulders are smoked daily here and pulled (not chopped) to order, which retains freshness and moisture and offers large bites of smoky crust. The saucy ribs and sweet beans were fine, but after one bite of the Brunswick stew my attention was solidly diverted. Maybe it was the stasis between soup and stew, or the kick of black pepper that this Texan is addicted to. It may have also been the solid smokiness of the meat within that stew, but the answer isn't as important as the discovery of my favorite Brunswick stew in Georgia.

The back roads I used to get to Dean's Barbeque (since 1947) proved inefficient and the clock was ticking quickly toward my departure time. Inside a Styrofoam container there was slaw and stew nearly equal in appearance and quality to what I found at Fresh Air, but the uniformly pale chunks of pork had been strangled beneath a pool of a sweet vinegar sauce. Every awful bite came with a vinegar chaser. Maybe the sandwich was better, but I had to hit a gas station before dropping the rental. Two out of three ain't bad.

November: Bill Addison convinced me to come a bit earlier so we could venture out to some of his favorites in Marietta just northwest of the city and outside the loop. We had grand plans of multiple stops that evening, but the Atlanta gridlock was too much to overcome. It gave us time to talk about the real possibility of becoming a writer. Bill listened eagerly as I explained my early negotiations with Texas Monthly. They had hinted at the possibility of taking me on as a writer—a barbecue writer. A hint was all I needed at that point.

We just beat the closing sign at Dave Poe's. It took only one bite of the pulled pork to know that it was some of the best in the state. Bill noted my audible moan after the first bite of the moist, smoky meat. Chicken wings flecked with a ruddy spice coating were crisp with a hint of sweetness. Ribs and brisket were forgettable while familiar cheesy pasta was less greasy than other versions, but the Brunswick stew had an oil slick on top. We were already late for the next stop.

DAVID KAMP is a writer and humorist whose work appears most frequently in *Vanity Fair*. He is the author of, among other books, *The United States of Arugula*, a chronicle of American food trends.

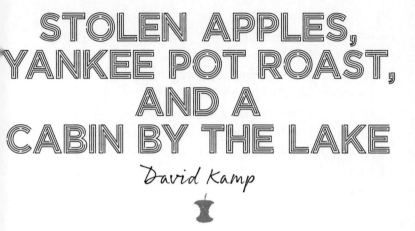

STOLEN APPLES, YANKEE POT ROAST, AND A CABIN BY THE LAKE

David Kamp

I still have the little printed card from the place:

MAPLE COTTAGE
FOR TOURISTS
'A Good Place to Spend the Night'
Cabins and Good Meals at Reasonable Rates

R.M. FLETCHER

Maple Cottage was a clapboard farmhouse on the outskirts of Center Harbor, New Hampshire, about ten miles east of Squam Lake, where Katharine Hepburn and Henry Fonda scenically confronted their mortality in the 1981 film *On Golden Pond*. It had been built, like most nineteenth-century farmhouses, close to the road, just a few feet back from New Hampshire Route 25.

Old people and transient guests, the ones just looking
for a place to bed down for a night, stayed in Maple Cottage
itself. We stayed in one of the cabins, which were a quarter
mile beyond the main house, down a dirt road in the back.
The cabins, white with green trim around the windows, were
spartan: bare bulbs for lights, knotty-wood walls, cold water
only, no bathtubs or showers. But they looked right onto a
secret little lake. Kanasatka, it was called: a kind of budget
version of Squam Lake/Golden Pond—much smaller, but
with the same blue crystallinity and families of warbling
loons skimming its surface at twilight. We did our bathing
and laving in its waters, using overturned Frisbees as floating
soap trays.

R.M. Fletcher was Robert Fletcher, 'Rob' to his old
friends—who, like him, were literally old—and 'Mr. Fletcher'
to my family. He was a lifelong bachelor, congenitally shy,
born and raised on the Maple Cottage property, back when it
had been a working farm. He had thick white hair barbered
in a tight 1920s style and the plain features of a Dorothea
Lange sharecropper. He was usually wearing an apron over
his short-sleeve dress shirt and belted trousers, because he
was usually in some stage of meal preparation.

I probably exchanged no more than two sentences ever
with Mr. Fletcher, but I was always overjoyed at the first sight
of him—that moment each year when our car pulled up at
Maple Cottage after the seven-hour drive from New Jersey.
My father would get out and enter the house through the side
door, where the kitchen was. A minute or so later, he and
the old man would emerge, engaged in jovial small talk. We

would all say our hellos to Mr. Fletcher and catch wafts of whatever was cooking inside. Sometimes it might be a baked good like apple pie or cranberry bread, but usually the air carried a gravy aroma. An inviting one, like the kind you wake up to on Thanksgiving.

⇥⥫

'Cabins and Good Meals at Reasonable Rates': truth in advertising. We were a Mom, a Dad, a girl, and two boys, and, for a two-figure sum per night, we got two squares a day, breakfast and dinner, and a beach more or less to ourselves, since none of Mr. Fletcher's other patrons seemed to love Lake Kanasatka as much as we did. We took our meals in the Maple Cottage dining room with our fellow guests, boarding-house-style. Breakfast was at 8am and dinner, 6pm. At mealtimes, Mr. Fletcher would summon us cabin-dwellers by standing on his porch and waving one of those town crier–type bells in the direction of the lake, *Ya-DING, Ya-DING*! Sometimes, if my brother and I charged up the dirt road fast enough, we would catch sight of the old man shuffling back into the house, his aproned back to us, his walk rickety and arthritic, the bell silent by his hip. He looked exactly like a codger in a George Booth cartoon in the *New Yorker*.

This was in the 1970s and early '80s. My father was a car salesman who got precisely two weeks of vacation time a year, and he always took the same two weeks off—the last two in August, leading up to Labor Day. I was aware that other kids my age were getting on airplanes and going to Disney World or family-owned condos in Florida, but not for a second did it ever occur to me that our vacations were modest or old-fashioned. As I learned later, though, our family's way was pretty much how working-class families had holidayed a century earlier. Norman Rockwell, in his memoir, *Norman Rockwell: My Adventures as an Illustrator*, describes childhood getaways from his native New York City (yes, he was a city kid, despite his totemic depictions of small-town life) that, though they took place when William McKinley was president, sound strikingly familiar:

> My family spent every summer until I was nine or ten years old in the country at various farms which took in boarders. Those country boardinghouses weren't like the resorts of today … Those boardinghouses were just farms. The grownups played croquet or sat in the high slat-backed rockers which lined the long front porch. We kids were left to do just about anything we wanted.

Mr. Fletcher's land was no longer being actively farmed, but the area remained farm country and the cuisine was still farmhouse—not so much in the 'farm to table' way of today's neo-retro agritourism, in which your married-couple 29-year-old innkeepers might present you with a fresh-plucked heritage pullet roasted with fingerlings and garlic scapes from the very acre upon which the dear bird foraged, but in the hearty, stick-to-your-ribs way that sustained farmers who had corn to thresh and hay to bale and cows to milk, and therefore required lots and lots of calories to burn.

Breakfast was two courses. Oatmeal first, served in a generous, undainty portion, with cream and brown sugar. The oatmeal was necessary, because late Augusts in New Hampshire carried with them a heavy intimation of fall, meaning not only that there were a few red maples along the road already beginning to turn, but also that the air temperature reliably plunged into the low forties at night. We'd wake up to vapor coming off the lake and out of our mouths. Though it would be swimming and canoeing weather by 11.15, it was sweatshirt and oatmeal weather at eight. After the oatmeal came the 'proper' breakfast, which, if syrup pitchers were set out on the table (my preferred scenario), was pancakes or French toast. Absent the syrup pitchers, it was piles of eggs with piles of toast and rashers of bacon.

But it was Mr. Fletcher's dinners that captivated me and have kept Maple Cottage forever in my mind. Unambitious and cost-conscious as my family might have been in terms of travel, we lived very much in thrall to the aspirational food manias of the times, whether that meant visiting the wondrous new places that Craig Claiborne and Mimi Sheraton told us about in the *New York Times* (Dean & DeLuca! The Fondue Pot!), or, at home, essaying Julia Child's *soupe au pistou* or Mollie Katzen's carrot-cashew curry. Perversely, Mr. Fletcher's stolid Yankee cooking, with its clean, uncomplicated flavors, struck me as radical.

Sundays only, he did a 'supper' at 1pm instead of six. It was basically the full Thanksgiving, expertly realized: the turkey, the stuffing, the cranberry sauce, and what have you. A day or two later, the leftover turkey would reappear in a pot pie with peas, root vegetables, and late-summer corn. It sounds ridiculous, but, prior to Maple Cottage, I had never heard of pot pie and was unaware in general of the concept of flaky crust–encased savories.

Mr. Fletcher's turkey pot pie blew my mind, as did his Yankee pot roast, as did his ritual Saturday-night New England boiled dinner: braised vegetables, brisket that he'd corned himself, baked beans, and, most exotically of all, circular slices of molasses-steeped New England brown bread, home-baked in a coffee can. Inasmuch as one can eat a Norman Rockwell painting, that's what I did, nightly and voraciously.

Dessert was a cake or fruit pie, Fletcher-made, never store-bought. One night, one of the old-timers with whom we shared a table, Aggie, asked me if I'd liked the apples in the apple pie. Aggie was a central-casting little old lady with pluck: gray hair up in a bun, floral-print summer dress. Years before we met her, she had lost her husband, 'my Joe', and she kept his memory alive by faithfully listening to his Red Sox on the radio. I told Aggie that yes, I'd liked the apples in the pie. 'What if I told you,' she asked, pausing for dramatic effect, 'that *they'd been stolen?*'

Aggie was herself the thief. On her daily constitutional, she had happened upon a tree on a neighbor's property that was already bearing ripe fruit, and she'd helped herself. Mr. Fletcher sheepishly acknowledged to us that he had accepted the goods even though they were hot.

Oftentimes after dinner, we would all—my family, Aggie, the other elderfolk roosting in the rooms upstairs, the hippie-hiker couples passing through in their Volkswagens—retire to the house's front parlor, where an upright piano stood. There, another of Mr. Fletcher's solo regulars, an Episcopal minister from Rhode Island named John Evans, who was somehow able to spend his entire summers at Maple Cottage, entertained us with song—not religious music but Tin Pan Alley stuff that he played off the top of his head or from the stacks of old sheet music that sat atop the piano. Reverend Evans was a multi-instrumentalist and a gabby, endearingly affable eccentric, a bit like *The Music Man*'s Professor Harold Hill but with actual musical ability. I still have his printed cards, too, five of 'em: one that describes him as a reverend, two that describe him as a harpist, one that describes him as 'Singer, Author', and another that describes him as 'Entertainer', his specialties being 'Country, Dixieland, Oldies'. He and my father, a gifted amateur crooner, got along like a house on fire and duetted by the piano until it got late, which, at Maple Cottage, was around 9.03pm. At that point, it was sweatshirts on, flashlights out, and back down the hill to the cabin by the lake.

To recap: I spent summer evenings in a country boarding house eating meals with strangers and listening contentedly as people merrily sang along to sheet music in the parlor. What century did I grow up in again?

I suspect that even then, as a child, a part of me recognized that what I was witnessing and participating in was a time warp, a way of life that already belonged to the past. I further suspect that this was part of the allure. Maple Cottage may not have been as glam a destination as the high-rise Florida condos or Colorado ski resorts to which my more affluent friends traveled, but it was every bit as transportive. Probably more so.

I've since gotten to take airplane trips and swim in tropical waters and bargain in souks and sleep in hotel suites whose nightly rack rates have run to four figures. Still, Maple Cottage remains the *beau idéal* of vacations in my mind, and I retain the provincial bias that there is nowhere in the world as pretty as New England in late summer. And while my palate has since been treated to hundreds of experiences putatively more exciting and broadening than the simple country meals prepared by that old man in his farmhouse in New Hampshire, my abiding culinary love is for the kind of congenial, familial New England home cooking where everything seems to be infused with either pie spices or pan drippings. 'Mr. Fletcher food,' I call it.

ANNABEL LANGBEIN is New Zealand's leading food writer and publisher, and the star of the TV series, Annabel Langbein: The Free Range Cook. Her 19 cookbooks have won numerous international awards and sold more than two million copies throughout Europe, North America, and Australasia. To find out more visit annabel-langbein.com.

THE RIGHT SIDE OF THE FALL LINE

Annabel Langbein

Dusk was falling, that swift folding of day into darkness that characterises the tropics. As the light condensed and dwindled I contemplated my ill planning. The fact that I would be arriving at my destination late into the night, with no bookings, no connections and no means of letting anyone know where I was seemed optimistic beyond belief. I had figured the bus trip from Rio to Ouro Preto to be around six hours but here I was with another four hours still to go. A thread of anxiety started its twist into my stomach as the bus wound ever onwards into the dense blackness of night.

The man sitting next to me on this endless journey was short and balding with a neatly trimmed beard. He wore a cable-knit cardigan and grey Velcro shoes ... strange how banal details like this can be recalled ... it certainly wasn't as if I fancied him. But he was a friendly enough companion to share the view from the front seat of the bus, revealing the nuances of the landscape along the way and, as the journey progressed, more personal details of his life. He was a policeman in Rio. He was making the trip to visit his recently widowed mother. He grew up in Ouro Preto and would be there for a few days over the fiesta of Nossa Senhora do Rosário. His name was Cynlio.

It was close to midnight when the bus finally rolled into the town square. Rain falling in buckets, the pitchest black of unwelcoming nights. My querulous enquiries to the bus driver in stumbling Portuguese—the whereabouts of a hotel, an information centre, a phone booth—were all met with a blank stare of incomprehension. Cynlio popped into my one-way conversation in his pidgin Portu-English, gently informing me there would be 'no thing open now, no hotel until *amanhã de manhã*'. In other words, tomorrow morning. But he had a 'good' solution. I could stay at his mother's house, with my own room at the front. I would be safe and she would not mind …

We are talking 1982 here, a time when Brazil was not known for its safety. That very day, as I left Rio, a radio report came on about a woman whose glittering bejeweled hand had been macheted off as she drove through town with the window open. No TripAdvisor, or Airbnb, no cell phones. No internet. A policeman in these parts could be a good guy or just as easily a bad guy.

I often think about the fall lines of life, the invisible tightropes that divide moments of calamity and serendipity. This was such a moment. Accepting the invitation of a bed from a stranger—would I get the axe murderer, or had I found myself a fabulous guide? It could have gone either way.

It seemed that my only other option would be to wander the pitch-black streets, and sleep in some doorway or roadside shelter. I had done that already in the wilderness of the Bolivian Altiplano, but in that case with the welcome company and friendship of three other hitchhikers. Right now, this option did not seem like any kind of good idea.

And so I set off with Cynlio, winding through narrow cobbled streets, head down into the malevolent night.

Cynlio's ancient mother was up waiting for him when we arrived, drenched to the skin at her doorstep. She seemed initially rather put out to see her beloved son with a blonde stranger in tow. But explanations were made, smiles were shared, and welcomes provided. I was led through the tiny hall to the front room and the smallest of rough beds, shown the humblest of bathrooms and left to change out of my cold wet clothes. On re-entering the living room, Cynlio declared we needed to go out right away to meet his friends. The axe murderer argument going on in my head had somewhat abated—if he was going to kill me, I figured it would have happened by now.

Only a policeman would know where the after-hours joints were open in this kind of a town. And a few paces from Cynlio's mother's doorway took us to another nondescript entrance, and with a couple of coded knocks we were let inside a buzzing bar. Cynlio's old schoolfriends crowded around, welcoming him back to the fold, regaling him with the stories of their lives over round after round of *cachaça* shots. If you haven't come across cachaça, it is created from sugar cane, is clear as water and with the kick of eighty per cent proof alcohol. In these parts of the world it was (and probably still is) the local panacea of choice. When life dishes up endless hardship and disappointment, cachaça delivers a necessary sense of fortitude, and paints a euphoric glow around its jagged edges.

It was around 4am when we all rolled out of the bar, the men drunk as fish. Their capacity for alcohol was extraordinary. Pasqual, the tall, elegant crooner of the group, announced there would be a feast in honour of my arrival and that we must all reconvene at his home at 2pm the next day.

I retired safely to my little bed in the front room with its raggedy sheets and thin holy blanket. Around noon I woke with a hangover to beat all hangovers—cachaça's warm hand of friendship is very short-lived. For breakfast—strong black coffee and another round of cachaça for all three of us, Cynlio's mother included. I was starting to get the gist, no hair of the dog round here, more like the full skin to keep everyone floating in a slightly glazed state, no matter the hour.

I had thought the whole idea of a feast was one of those drunken moments everyone would forget in the clear light of a new day. But no, we were off, hurrying not to be late, Pasqual was a *very* good cook …

Pasqual's house was, in fact, a bit of a shack set on the side of a hill a ways out of town. I remember ripening coffee beans hanging down the banks, and masses of wild orchids. It had stopped raining but the air was still heavy and the sky dark and threatening. In the freshness of day the group made a motley bunch—apart from Pasqual, the rest looked like street people, roughly dressed vagabonds in short order: the tall, morose, skinny man; the coal-black man with hard miner's hands and rope muscles of arms and legs; the short fat man; a younger skinny kid who looked like he had come out of the army (camo attire noted); and of course our host, lean and tawny-skinned, with a near perfect grasp of English, and a voice smooth as butter, Pasqual. Out came a bottle of cachaça, drinks were poured and plans laid.

The miner was dispatched to get firewood. The tall morose chap was sent for his guitar, the army kid was told to find alcohol (by what means I shall never know as no one in this renegade bunch appeared to have a bean between them) and the short fat one headed off to find the women—who I was told would help clean up and be great for the dancing and 'after'. I didn't enquire further.

Two ancient fowls were caught from the yard and dispatched out of sight. While this was happening the crew gradually reassembled with their contributions; the women, we were told, would all be there around 6pm. By 4pm the fire was lit, and the new bottle of cachaça opened and emptied. Outside, on a wooden block near the fire, Pasqual chopped onions and garlic. The chicken was cut into large chunks and all the blood from both birds sat in a dirty old enamel jug. Throughout proceedings this jug was repeatedly raised and toasted to us, his audience. 'Here lies the soul of my dish,' Pasqual proclaimed. 'Today I make my famous *frango ao molho pardo*.' At this stage things weren't looking either impressive or appetising. I started wondering how I was going to get out of this meal in order to avoid chronic food poisoning.

But it was time to start cooking. A vast iron pot was set on the fire, some oil went in and the chunks of bird browned, onions and garlic added, along with freshly picked bay leaves and oregano, a chilli or two and some black peppercorns. As soon as everything started to sizzle hard, lots of water was added to the pot along with a small handful of salt. Once it all came to the boil, the jug of blood was mixed with a little vinegar and a little cornmeal and stirred into the stew. The embers were loosened to drop the heat and this huge pot left to simmer slowly for the next couple of hours, while we went on to drink some more cachaça. By this stage, four buxom women had arrived—tightly topped and highly made up, they were a lot older than they would have liked me believe. The guitar came out and the melancholy in its strummer's face fell away as if he was in the arms of a lover; the young boy was dispatched for another alcohol raid, and Pasqual turned his attention to the rest of our meal. Heading into the small makeshift kitchen inside his shack he retrieved a large jar of polenta. Water was boiled in another giant heavy iron pot over a gas burner inside; the polenta rained in and swirled to a simmer, then was left to plop for another hour or so. Back outside it was now completely dark, the sky was clear and everyone was getting very drunk. The heartwarming scent of the stew drifted on a soft breeze of jasmine. The effect was transporting, a fleeting moment when nothing could be bad in the world.

It was around 8pm when our feast was finally declared '*pronto agora*'. A pile of tin plates was assembled by the fire with a rough collection of forks and spoons, a table quickly constructed with an old door, more blocks of wood pulled up as seats and some candles lit to break the darkness. The now creamy polenta was ladled onto the plates, and this most fragrant of deep brown chicken stews spooned on top. In their hours of slow cooking over the fire those two bony old birds had sacrificed every inch of their flavour to the pot, their scraggly flesh was now rendered succulently tender, and the blood, which I had looked at with such horror, had filled out every corner of the sauce with a deep dark richness. The subtle tonings of herbs, the hint of chilli and the smoky flavour of the fire brought everything together in the most perfect balance. From so little Pasqual had created a truly magnificent dish. Against the creaminess of the polenta it was just *soooo* good. For about ten minutes there was silence but for the chirp of crickets, as each of us disappeared into a private reverie of gustatory bliss.

I felt like I had stumbled into my own Steinbeck novel. Here in this wild place, eating the best chicken stew in the world with a bunch of vagabonds hard on their luck. In that humble stew, beyond the pleasures of taste, there was so much else to savour. Its essence held so many of the things it takes to make a good life—resourcefulness, pride and care, a connectedness to nature, and the pleasures of a meal shared together around the table—most of the means to transform a life of raw poverty and grinding hardship.

The power of friendship and camaraderie, music and laughter, a day and a night of good times created out of little more than two tough old fowls and a crapped-out guitar. I guess you have to give the cachaça some credit as well.

→))→

A few days later I got back to Rio feeling less than ordinary, and wearing a wild rash. The doctor looked me over. 'Ahh,' he mused, 'you have been bitten by our devil drink cachaça … You are a very lucky girl that it didn't kill you.'

On the right side of the fall line, but precariously close to the precipice.

ALAN RICHMAN is a long-time food writer who has won 11 James Beard journalism awards for restaurant reviewing. He frequently angers people, but never before have they been Egyptians.

OMAR SHARIF SLEPT HERE

Alan Richman

It's late summer in Cairo, less than a year after the rise of the Arab Spring, and I'm off to watch a protest at Tahrir Square, a celebrated venue for disparaging local government. On the schedule: a 1pm demonstration against military trials for civilians. Who wouldn't be against that?

My only concern is whether I will have time beforehand for lunch at a nearby koshary—koshary being the national dish of Egypt. Inasmuch as I am a food writer and not a news reporter, meals tend to take priority, but perhaps not at this moment. An opportunity to observe firsthand the most expansive political movement in the Middle East since the Ottoman Empire replaced the Byzantine is difficult to resist.

I am here as a kind of culinary anthropologist, someone who delves into restaurants the way more learned men, Egyptologists, peer into pyramids. They study the way the ancients lived; I look at how modern society eats. Nothing is more transparent than a restaurant, where little except the kitchen is hidden from view.

The Arab Spring has remained to this point relatively levelheaded, which uprisings rarely do. Nevertheless, I have been warned to stay clear of Tahrir Square by young professionals I met at a dinner in Lebanon, just before departing for Cairo. Actually, they advised me to stay away from the whole city, cancel my visit because the police had abandoned their posts and the streets were out of control. You have to admit, when residents of a city like Beirut claim they're frightened of someplace other than where they live, a sensible fellow takes note.

I feel no unease as I walk out of my hotel, located in Zamalek, a residential district on a small island in the middle of the Nile. Life on this spit of land is considered upscale by locals, but that doesn't mean much. Living conditions in Cairo peaked nearly a hundred years ago.

My confidence in the civility of the dissenters is reinforced when I cross the bridge onto the mainland and walk past vendors selling snacks and keepsakes. If I've learned anything in life, it's that menace is rarely encountered in the presence of popcorn. My sense of well-being grows as I come closer. The vendors are offering Egyptian flags and T-shirts with dates commemorating the uprising against Hosni Mubarak, the former president. For sale are multicolored pom-poms whose purpose eludes me, although the presence of cheerleaders would add an additional level of friendliness to Tahrir Square.

I happen upon Mohammad Abdel Kairm, standing on the sidewalk outside his small souvenir and gift shop. He informs me that he used to live in Kew Gardens, a section of New York City's Queens, and adds, 'This is much safer than New York, I'm telling you.'

He says the latest troubles are being brought on not by protestors but by the police, who are paying people to cause trouble so that all Egyptians will cry out for the police and the military to return and save the country. As I leave his shop I inadvertently step on prayer rugs that have been spread out on the narrow, well-trod sidewalk. I immediately act contrite, not like a typical New Yorker who might complain that the rugs have no business being strewn along a busy corridor. The men who have placed them there immediately start yelling, but not at me. They are irritated at the shop owner for not warning me that I was about to walk over them.

In the square I see freshly baked sweet potatoes, cooked over coals, ordinarily irresistible but not on a summer day so brutally hot even the Great Sphinx is toweling himself off. Pushing, shoving, jostling, deliriously happy people are everywhere, climbing on everything in sight but leaving a wide ring of empty space around the potatoes, which are radiating a near-nuclear core of heat. I feel privileged to be at the epicenter, at least for one day, of this exhilarating and impulsive expression of democracy that is electrically racing through the Muslim world.

Although the square is already bursting, I am slightly early for the 1pm commencement of events. The timing of the start is indicative of local respect for religious traditions—Friday is a weekly holy day, when services begin around noon and generally are over by 1pm. I must decide. Only two blocks away is Koshary El Tahrir, which is to koshary what Nathan's on Coney Island is to hot dogs. Since I'm early, I alter course and make my way there. I'm hungry, and yet another bit of wisdom I've picked up over the years is that it's never smart to miss a meal.

The watchful owner of the undersized establishment, never still, leads me to a table for two, already occupied by one. Across from me is a young man who has completed his meal but does not get up to leave as I sit down. He is too polite to do so. I quickly realize that he speaks English, so I ask him if he minds sharing his table. He introduces himself as Mahmoud Abozied and replies, 'We are friendly here. We share everything.'

My bowl of food comes with a spoon and a cup, very army field mess. Everything is modern, which isn't commonplace in Cairo. Koshary can vary somewhat, but here I see crunchy, toasted pasta—the textural heart of the concoction—plus rice, lentils, chickpeas and fried onions. It is possibly the least-expensive restaurant food on earth, with a small plastic bowl selling for less than a dollar.

The standard accompaniments are two sauces, one vinegary and the other peppery. I pick up the red bottle and the friendly fellow says, 'Be careful with the pepper. It is hot like hell.' He would make a fine food critic, because I am soon gasping. Egypt does not have a particularly fiery cuisine, and I thought he was exaggerating.

I thank him for warning me and compliment him on his culinary brilliance.

'I am not brilliant. I am Egyptian,' Abozied says.

I try the second sauce, the mild one.

'Is it good?' he asks.

'Delicious,' I say, meaning it.

'It is cheap food,' he says. 'It is not poor food. Egyptians are simple people. We do not have a typical society rat race after money. We want safety. We have a common statement: "If you are in your house and have food, you own the world." It is strange but true.'

He tells me that he is a financial consultant, which intrigues me, inasmuch as this appears to be a country without money. I ask him for a prediction of the future of Egypt.

'We are in a mess,' he says.

Then he leaves for Tahrir Square, a plain man trying to better his country, very American Revolution to me.

The food of Egypt, I will soon learn, is unsophisticated, unruly, inexpensive and totally cherished by Egyptians. Ingredients are combined in ways I cannot comprehend, and, for that matter, some of the most revered products are themselves off-putting. You'd think even an Egyptian epicure would tire of *mulukhiyi*, a not particularly toothsome green leaf that continually pops up in dishes. Basically, it is an uncomfortable cuisine for anyone who has not lived all his life here. Nobody comes to Egypt for the cuisine, except perhaps me.

A week of eating passes before I become discouraged by the restaurants, Koshary El Tahrir being easily the most satisfying. However, all it takes is one day in the city, September 9, 2011, for me to be stripped of my hope for the Arab Spring. Everything my friends in Beirut had warned me about came true.

That night, long after I had left Tahrir Square, protestors marched on the Israeli Embassy, an act of infamy. Three Egyptians were killed by security forces, and the scaredy-cat Israeli ambassador fled the country. (Moshe Dayan, Israeli war hero, would have wept.) I never was in danger from the embassy riot, didn't even realize it had occurred until the next day. And while this was not the first Arab Spring event to turn violent, it did set a standard for senselessness.

I never stopped enjoying Cairo. At no time did I feel uncomfortable there, no matter where I wandered, and I went everywhere in search of a good meal. I was often lost. Away from the primary thoroughfares, the city is a jumble of unmarked or badly marked streets. Maps aren't much help.

Walking around means constantly dodging cars as you cross streets. No drivers stop willingly for pedestrians, although they do honk incessantly. As I walked along sidewalks, I was splattered with water dripping from leaky overhead air-conditioners. I splashed through puddles of staggering biological implications—they were certainly not water, not when it hadn't rained in a week. Much of Cairo is like any other poor city—tiny shops, some no larger than one-car garages, pressed up against each other; concertina wire protecting empty lots; plastic tables and chairs set out on sidewalks so friends can eat, drink, play cards and smoke the hookah. (Non-validated tip: Ask for your hookah 'Egyptian', and you might receive a sprinkling of hash.) I always feel alive when I walk along streets such as these. Maybe it's because I'm usually alone in my travels and the crush of pedestrians is a substitute for company.

The unpredictability and diversity of the restaurants is unquestionably fascinating, although I am wary when I visit a city and find restaurants that offer foreign food primarily for one reason: they're safe havens for tourists who distrust the cuisine of the countries they're visiting. Egypt certainly meets that criterion. Nevertheless, I was eager to try La Trattoria, owned by Tarek Sharif, son of the famous Egyptian actor Omar Sharif. I had heard that he ate there frequently, but he wasn't on hand the evening I showed up. In fact, only one table was occupied.

The décor was minimalistic, stark, very Ingmar Bergman. The one bit of art was a mounted poster promoting Italian wines, although the restaurant offered none. A young, dour waiter glanced at me, picked up a menu, and shuffled to the rear of the room, not even looking back to see if I was following. He silently pointed to a seat. I took it, feeling as though I had been relegated to detention hall. The space was airless. And peopleless. I sat, waited. A few more tables filled up, near the front. I remained alone.

The waiter ultimately returned and placed a knife and fork in front of me. They pointed in different directions. He put a cloth napkin in front of a different chair, one where I clearly wasn't sitting. I ordered a selection of appetizers. Vitello tonnato—roasted veal with a creamy tuna sauce—was the highlight of my meal. It almost convinced me that the cook had knowledge of Italian food. The skewered baked shrimp were crunchy. The mozzarella was impossibly hard, but excellent compared to the spaghetti pomodoro, which was tragic.

I understand why Omar Sharif is a steady customer. The despair of *Doctor Zhivago*, his greatest film, is mirrored in the bleakness of his son's restaurant.

Less ambitious than La Trattoria, but even more disappointing, was Lucille's, subject of a 2007 story by *Time* magazine with the headline, 'The World's Best Hamburger Is In Egypt'. I wanted very much to believe. Lucille's is very Johnny Rockets. The menu is plasticized, a facsimile of the kind found in chain restaurants. It has photos and a credo: '… we mix and grind our own ground beef to give you the best quality there's no better way to do it!'

Friends and I ordered burgers, of course. The buns were oversized and spongy, and dwarfed the miniature portion of meat within. The meat itself tasted like the kind you get in supermarkets when you buy chopped meat on special, cook it, and wonder why it doesn't taste much like beef. I'm not saying Lucille's has the world's worst hamburger—I'm not as impetuous as *Time*—but it's in the running for the title.

The concierge of my hotel kept urging me to try a nearby pizzeria, Maison Thomas. When he gave me the address, I realized it was the same as two other restaurants already on my list of places to try. That was puzzling until I realized that all three were attached in different ways to the same building, a monolithic relic of old Cairo that was so huge, so spread out, so battered and so gnarly I wouldn't have been surprised to learn it had a root system. It even had a name, Baehler's Mansions, after a hotelier and developer prominent in Cairo in the early 1920s.

Maison Thomas was in the front, on the main thoroughfare, and easy to find. Abou El Sid, famous for traditional Egyptian cuisine, was toward the rear, behind a huge, black Temple of Doom door. La Bodega turned out to be above me, on the second floor. The building boasted an ancient cage elevator leading up to it, but the elevator didn't work. I wondered when last it had.

I had lunch at La Bodega—such an odd name for a place serving French and Continental Cuisine. It looked more like a private club than a restaurant, one King Farouk might have patronized, although I later learned that it wasn't quite old enough for that. The dining room was glamorous, with vestiges of grandeur. The walls were the color of oxidized white wine. The bar was mostly brass. The wood trim was painted black. The flatware was heavy.

I was the only person in the room at lunch, which I believed would guarantee attentive service. I was wrong. I asked my indifferent waiter for shrimp flambéed tableside, which was on the menu, but he shook his head. I never knew why, although it might be a dish not offered when the temperature outside reaches ninety-five degrees Fahrenheit. He suggested beignet of salmon, which turned out to be a cross between a samosa and a spring roll, light and fresh but more like a snack than an appetizer in an elegant and expensive restaurant. For my main course, he was insistent that I have chicken tagine, served Moroccan style. The white meat was overcooked and served in a light, innocuous cream sauce. Couscous, the Moroccan touch, came on the side.

Maison Thomas offered a startling range of pizzas. Someone with considerable imagination had conceived them, given that both the Hawaii and the Monaco featured smoked roast beef, which I doubt is a staple of either locale. The mozzarella was impressively gooey, but the crust was so flat, pale and flavorless I was reminded of the unleavened bread that the Jews took out of Egypt when they fled a few thousand years ago.

The best feature of Abou El Sid, it turned out, was that magnificent door. If only it had remained locked. Inside, this classic restaurant resembled a haunted house, the mood enhanced by an occasional screeching sound, which was either a banshee or a blender gone berserk. I tried all manner of dishes, including a green soup containing *mulukhiyi* leaves (oddly medicinal), liver prepared Alexandria-style (overcooked and flavorless), and a pudding called keshk (reminiscent of cold, sweet, gooey cream of wheat). The wine, made in Egypt, was marked up in the manner of New York, which means four times its store price. I finished only one dish, the lentil soup, slightly too garlicky but otherwise without flaw.

I often imagined what dining in Cairo must have been like a hundred years ago, when the city was a place of grandeur. There isn't much of that splendor left, except in the near-ruins of still-occupied residential buildings and in some of the better international hotels. By far the most refined meal I ate was a Turkish dinner at the Kempinski Hotel. Let others wonder how the pharaohs could have built pyramids using twenty-ton blocks of stone. I can't understand how a people whose civilization predates all others couldn't come up with tastier food.

I wondered if the centuries-long dominance of the Ottoman Empire had somehow muddled a promising Egyptian cuisine. All manner of culinary influences would have been introduced, and it's possible that local cooks had the bad judgment to embrace the wrong ones. On the other hand, I might have expected too much from the food. Egypt is about ninety-five percent desert land. That doesn't leave much space for growing crops or grazing livestock.

An Egyptian-American teacher and writer suggested to me that Egypt's culinary descent was no different from what has occurred in all aspects of life there—the stifling of cultural, societal and intellectual standards. She said all had been stunted by the kind of oppression that led to the Arab Spring uprising. I can see why koshary, a profoundly simple dish that came into existence in the nineteenth century to feed poor working families, has survived intact. Its sturdy goodness is impervious to change.

JOSH OZERSKY is a James Beard Award-winning food writer. His work has appeared in *New York* magazine, *Time, Esquire, Saveur,* and *The Wall Street Journal.* He lives in New York City.

A MELANCHOLIC'S GUIDE TO EATING IN PARIS

Josh Ozersky

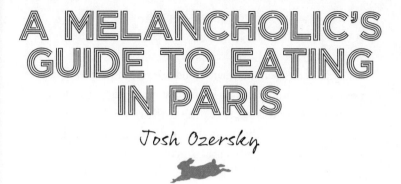

My father's attachment to raw wheat bran was unnatural, yes, and in some ways even masochistic, but it made sense if you knew what his diet was like. Not that it helped any. He had strange ideals of austerity that had almost no connection with what was going on inside his body. An example: for my entire childhood, he insisted on making me drink sour, grayish-green grapefruit juice, on the basis that it was 'less fattening' than sweet, delicious orange juice. I was to find out years later that they were almost identical; it was merely the badness of the former that appealed to him. Bran was a similarly penitential agent. He consumed Chinese spare ribs, blackened steaks, salami sandwiches, sausage pizzas, and every kind of wurst he could get his hands on, generally while standing in front of the refrigerator, or over the sink. He also drank prodigiously. He

was charismatic, loquacious, and unpredictable. So when I
got the news that we were going to Paris, I wasn't at all sure
what to expect.

My father's fascination with food was one of the few fixed
points of my childhood. A gifted painter, he produced a long
series of enormously expressive semi-abstract oil paintings
of chefs; I still have them and they make me feel very happy,
which would have pleased him, since he considered his
daily life as more or less their waste products. A melancholy
person, he was rarely cheered by anything, but food was one
thing that could be counted upon to get him excited. He was
never happier than when contemplating a take-out menu.
For my part, an only child raised among depressives, these
occasional flashes of light seemed like a much bigger deal
than they were, but then, food and movies were just about
the only things we were able to speak freely about. This was
especially true in my teenage years, when we lived together,
in a state of deep gloom interspersed with bursts of glee, in
our Atlantic City apartment. I was eighteen when I first heard
about the trip. Was it possible that he could stay happy for the
whole time?

It wasn't that far-fetched a possibility. My father had read
Liebling as a young man, and loved to quote from *Between
Meals*, much of which he had, he thought, committed to
memory. The book is a rhapsody of gluttony, set in the Paris
of the Lost Generation, although Liebling didn't know it
at the time. Like my father, he was primarily concerned
with eating, and, like my father, so much so that he would
spend hours pondering menus. I never read it myself, it

being boring-looking, but I loved it vicariously through my father, who used to say, 'Tonight, we're gonna ring the gong!' whenever he felt exceptionally excited about an imminent meal. The phrase derived, he said, from a story in *Between Meals*, when a young Liebling went into a fancy restaurant and used the phrase, an idiom he had learned in a book somewhere. Nobody understood what he was saying, and he later found out that the expression was one that hadn't been common since the seventeenth century. My father fell in love with it in that random way of his, though, and the words, 'we're going to ring the gong', persist in my own foodie patter, for reasons no one can understand. It's something of a private joke I have with myself.

The prospect of going to Paris with my father was special for another reason: it would be the longest period I had spent with him since becoming self-aware, sometime around the age of fifteen. My father, a stagehand at Resorts International Hotel Casino, worked a four-to-midnight shift, so was almost never home when I got back from school; my exposure to him, his strange flights of humor, his movie quotes, his sad expressions, his hidden emotions and obscure past, all came pretty much a few hours at a time. He kept a small bottle of vodka in the egg compartment and refused to eat fudge. I didn't understand him, but I wanted to be like him. I was curious what he would be like in Paris.

As it turned out, he was pretty much himself in Paris, only more so. While we did visit a few cultural touchstones, some of which even prompted a rare nugget of art history insight from him, mostly we were killing time between meals. I stood with him at the Rodin museum, contemplating The Thinker. He looked at it for a long time. I hoped he might say something smart and deep, something I could parrot in the presence of my friends. Instead, I got a predictable joke, one that made me laugh anyway. 'Should I get the steak or the cassoulet?' he asked in what he imagined would be the statue's voice. Our hotel, the small but elegant Claude Bernard, with its phone-booth elevator sheathed by a spiraling staircase, was the kind of place a man might shoot his cuffs and meet his mistress. As a rube, I was naturally awed by it, but within fifteen minutes, our clothes were lying around, my father had a small bottle of vodka on the bedside table, and there was a box of bran in the bathroom. It wasn't a bowl of bran, or a container of bran; it was the actual box, transported from our refrigerator, with a spoon from room service thrust into it. The idea was that we would eat so much rich food that the bran would provide the needed 'roughage' to keep our bowels in good working order. This was less than glamorous. It sat there for the whole trip. I felt that we were not a good fit in Paris. I told my father that there was a water fountain in the bathroom. 'Women use that to clean their twats,' he explained to me in that mordant way.

My dad's joke about steak vs. cassoulet was more relevant than he knew. Cassoulet was a familiar theme to me at the time, and one of the many disappointments of the trip. From my dutiful reading of Liebling, I had arrived in France ready for a cassoulet epiphany. I had even read in my father's dank copy of Waverly Root's *The Food of France* that there were not one, but three cassoulets that defined the regions of France, one from someplace that used only pork; another, from a place called Carcassonne, that also added mutton, which sounded great; and finally the celebrated Toulouse version, which had all that stuff, plus sausages and duck that had been simmered in its own fat. That sounded awesome, which made it all the more depressing when the reality turned out to be a dollop of tasteless white beans adorned with a few pieces here and there of sausage and salt pork. Cassoulet, at least in the form I got it, turned out to be essentially an unsauced version of franks and beans.

This discovery was part of a larger, more depressing reality that had nothing to do with my father. My problem in Paris was that, while I had thoroughly and eagerly internalized all his food propaganda about the place, I didn't actually like anything there. It wasn't simply, as with the grapefruit juice, his perverse preference for everything that was bad; it was simply that I had no point of reference for salads with raw eggs in them, or bony quails that required careful dissection to eat, or monstrous saucer-sized oysters like the one I was forced to eat at Vivarois. Everywhere I went I got steak frites, or something like it. I knew I disappointed my father, but there was nothing I could do about it. My upbringing had prioritized grilled cheese and bacon sandwiches, portly cheesesteaks, slabs of cake and, best of all, crusty, greasy hash browns cooked impatiently at the bottom of a pot. (Somehow, we had lost all the pans.)

Still, we did eat a lot. The Claude Bernard functioned as a staging area for our twice-a-day forays, from which we inevitably returned, bloated and woozy, by foot. These walks are my happiest memories of the trip. We were full, my father was in a good mood, it was just the two of us, and we enjoyed that special satori that only true gluttons know, of reconnoitering restaurants for the morrow while still full from dinner. 'You could eat great for the whole trip without leaving the block,' he would say, awestruck. We did in fact leave the block: we went to Moulin a Vent, on Rue des Fossés Saint-Bernard, a meatery with oil paintings of steak on the walls and a stout, butcherly looking waiter named Gilbert, who was amused to see us eat together. We went to the Select, to be like Hemingway, but it was just another coffee shop, although I had my first croque monsieur there, a French version of grilled cheese and bacon. We went to a more formal, less enjoyable restaurant called Chez Marius, which had an unctuous maître d' who looked a lot like *Hogan's Heroes* star Bob Crane. 'Bob Crane wasn't at his best tonight,' he told me apologetically, after a disappointing meal. But the best of the big meals was in fact just a few blocks away, and a big reason I still like to go back to 'the fifth': a small family restaurant called Moissonier.

Lacking any French, I assumed Moissonier was some kind of technical term—maybe the kitchen functionary charged with making mousse?—but it was in fact a guy named Louie Moissonier, who ran a homey, countrified restaurant with his wife Olamp, who had the blackest hair I have ever seen on any person, before or since. Moissonier was the first restaurant in Paris that made sense to me, registering as it did as an analog of the mom-and-pop Italian restaurants that I frequented in Atlantic City, like Angelo's Fairmont Tavern and The Derby. Every meal I have ever had at Moissonier, and I have had a lot, proceeded the same way. First came a cart filled with various cold things: garlicky sausages, potato salad and two dozen other items, none of which included vegetables. Then came an unmarked bottle of beaujolais wine from somebody's yard, and that was followed by a huge plate of chicken in a creamy vinegar sauce, and—and get this—*a giant black pan filled with crusty, cheesy brown potatoes.* 'There's your hash browns,' my father said, with an affectionate twist of mockery. I was oblivious to the comment, falling into the meal like a damaged airplane landing on one wheel. I still eat it whenever I can, and not just for nostalgic purposes. Those pans looked like they had been cast sometime during the War of the Spanish Succession; their craggy blackness was an unforgettable sizzling abyss.

It's telling that the potato gratin was such a high point in the trip; although we were set in an exotic locale, what with the Second Empire architecture, delicious ham sandwiches, and foxy, sharp-featured Sorbonne co-eds, the only things I was capable of enjoying were those that echoed my narrow, neurotic routines at home. My father and I watched movies in Atlantic City; in Paris we watched the same movies in the *version originale*, in art-house cinemas off the Rue des Écoles. I rejoiced in the pork sandwiches of South Philadelphia; the lamb sandwiches cut from slowly rotating spiked wads in the twisting alleys of San Severin were just a better version of that, with pungent salty-gamey meat slowly seared and self-basted over hours and then laid on a fresh crisp baguette and piled with fresh, crispy French fries. For my father, who never ran out of proofs that the French were better than us as a people, this was one more: 'Only they would know that you wanted French fries on top of your sandwich!' I would leave the hotel sometimes while he was napping, open-mouthed, on the bed, and make my way down the hill to the maze of magic shawarma, where I would follow the 'lambarinth', as I thought of it, past dozens of indistinguishable wad-men, until I came to my guy, a small, intense-looking man with a waxed moustache. (It was two francs for the sandwich, with either fries or salad on top, as if anyone would be dumb enough to choose salad.)

Louie Moissonier's pan of potatoes and the lambarinth were the high points of that trip, spectacles I vividly described to my friends when I got back, at almost nauseating length. But there were parts of the trip I never told anyone about, and tried not to remember myself. There was the night that we walked home and saw two glum-looking men sitting at a table outside a cafe, looking abjectly bored and depressed. They didn't speak at all. When we passed them, I said to my dad, 'Those guys are like, "Oh well, only another two hours to kill."' 'Only another thirty years to kill is more like it,' came his glum reply, and something seized up inside me. There was also the time he got all bombed and started crying. It was, I will say now in retrospect, very hard to have been put in such close quarters with a being as filled with despair as my father was in those years. I can hardly blame him—it sucks to come home one night from work and find that your wife has committed suicide—but I wish he could have been a little more in the spirit of the trip, bran aside. I think of him often, and the strangely stilted, but loving, relationship we had, and how we spoke the secret language of food as a proxy for everything else. He's gone now, along with my lamb wads, and so much more, but the paintings are still around. And every time I look at them I feel the urge to 'ring the gong'.

BETH KRACKLAUER is the food editor of the Off Duty section at *The Wall Street Journal*. Before that, she was an editor at the magazines *Gourmet* and *Saveur*. A native of Pittsburgh, Pennsylvania, she now lives in Brooklyn, New York.

THE IMPORTANCE OF CHICKEN LIVERS

Beth Kracklauer

We all enter our families in the middle of the action, and each of us is left to piece together our own story-in-progress as best we can. I would argue that for a youngest child, particularly one like me, born long after my siblings and even longer after my cousins—"not an accident, just a surprise!" has always been my mom's cheerful spin on the situation—this drama is, if not especially acute, then at least especially self-conscious. The dream where you find yourself on stage without a script? The gathering dread that your cue is approaching, and you're going to botch it? The only thing for it is to listen harder, watch more closely, will the action around you to coalesce into something intelligible. You read into things. Anyway, I do.

For instance, the fact that my father puts together a beautiful plate of food. I was well into adulthood before

I noticed; I recall the exact moment, in fact. It was in Kentucky, about an hour's drive southwest of Louisville, at the annual barbecue held by Dad's mother's relatives, the McCrackens and the Lancasters. That stretch of rolling farmland nestled up against the Ohio River is uncannily picturesque in places; our cousin Larry's farm is one of them. It sits on a hill and around a bend in the road in such a way that, on the approach, a perfect storybook spread unfolds: white farmhouse with peaked roof, a line of shade trees, fields planted in leafy green rows, more unobstructed sky than you ever see in a city.

We stepped out of the car and into the soup that is July in Kentucky. Languid in the humidity and the resinous haze of hickory smoke, ladies were draped over lawn chairs, drawling out their vowels only slightly, the way they do down there just below the Mason-Dixon. Kids, with that eerie energy that always makes a hot day seem hotter, hurled water balloons at each other and took turns cranking the churn on the ice-cream bucket. The men had just removed the pig, trussed up in chicken wire, from the smoker, a blackened behemoth engineered from a metal garbage dumpster by Larry, his uncle Bob, and some of the other guys. The smoker is fitted with rubber tires and a trailer hitch so they can haul it between their houses. This was the first year they'd had to purchase a pig to put in it. None of the families was raising them anymore; most of them had given up farming altogether.

A rotating team had tended the smoker through the night, and we'd brought along a couple of cases of beer to thank them. It was the best we could do, given that we'd spent the day before driving down from Pittsburgh, where I grew up and my parents still live. As we were hustled over to the long tables groaning under all the vegetable side dishes and salads and fresh fruit and fruit pies our relatives' gardens could supply, our own contribution felt pretty sorry. It always did. I remember being quietly amazed, years ago, when cousin Denise told me she'd not only made the smoky, slow-cooked beans, but also the ketchup that went into them. (Didn't ketchup come from Heinz?)

'You're just a house flower, aren't you?' said cousin Mary Ann to a visibly wilted me as we sat down with our plates of food. The truth is, I am a sort of alien life form in that context. My hometown is a no-nonsense, Northern, rust-belt city where people put their french fries right on their sandwiches because, well, why not? My parents transplanted themselves far from any extended family before they started their own. To gain entry to this tribe once a year on our visits to Kentucky always felt exciting, and also a little like crashing a party at a late hour, by which point so much has already happened it seems impossible to catch up and fall into the easy rapport everyone else has already established. (That dream again: Where's my script? What's my cue?)

For my dad, it's different. He has a lived history in this place; he spent summers with the elder members of this clan, back when they were all kids. It's funny to see quirks I tend to think of as uniquely Fred Kracklauer reflected back to me in a whole crowd of people. Wisecracking. Given to arguing, and to relishing it. And very intense about food. I've already mentioned the custom-built smoker that looms like an altar over each of these gatherings. The spread these people put out—its vastness and variety—is overwhelming. The unreserved pleasure they take in eating it is palpable.

I think I can be forgiven, then, for getting a little emotional, a little existential, even, when I looked over at my dad's plate. I was actually moved to capture it on film, and can therefore report that the elegant composition consisted of, beginning at the top and going clockwise, cucumber and onion salad, red potato salad dotted with mustard seeds, coleslaw, a pile of rosy pulled pork with just a dab of sticky sauce, barbecued beans, a salad of juicy tomatoes flecked with herbs, and another of fresh raspberries, blueberries and peaches. Giddy abundance, but selected and arranged with such care. That judicious dab of sauce. It takes a complicated history of loss and longing and seeking out the place where you feel safe to put together a plate like that.

❧

My dad made his first trip to Kentucky at the age of two-and-a-half. Up to then, the only world he knew was the Teutonic Midwest—Milwaukee, Wisconsin—where his Southern, Irish-Catholic mother had settled among her husband's German-immigrant family. It was the spring of 1936, and my grandmother, shattered by the death of an infant son she'd only just delivered, had to be hospitalized. For whatever reason, no relatives were able to take in little Fred and his five-year-old sister, Joann. Now, Joann was a well-behaved girl whom various neighbors were only too happy to watch over for a while. But Fred had already developed a reputation. Wisecracking. Given to arguing. Etc.

And so my grandmother's sister Elsie, then a footloose young student nurse, boarded a train in Louisville along with her friend Belle and headed north to collect her nephew. The two young ladies made a big impression. Belle, Dad recalls, always carried a penknife. She had a trick he never tired of, where she'd 'swallow' the knife (and let it drop down the front of her dress). I can remember Aunt Elsie in later years, shaking with laughter as she told the one about how young Fred pulled himself up on his seat and entertained the whole train carriage with a saucy song his father had taught him, 'Two Old Maids in a Folding Bed'. At last, an appreciative audience!

Fred stayed through the summer with another of his mother's sisters, Mae, and her husband, Ed, on their farm near the edge of Fort Knox. Once his mother had recovered and he'd returned to Wisconsin, he often headed back to that farm again come summer. Aunt Mae was known for having little patience for children. She and Uncle Ed had none of their own, and she wasn't keen on Fred socializing too much with his cousins. Well, she must have been saving up all her patience for him, because, as my dad remembers it, he was lavished with attention and affection. As a little boy, he'd ride on Uncle Ed's lap for hours as he drove the hay rake pulled by Kate the mule. Later, when Fred was eight or nine years old and interested in smoking cigarettes like his cousins were, Aunt Mae packed a corncob pipe with dry leaves, and the two of them sat and smoked together.

'Oh, Aunt Mae made such nice food,' Dad always says. Pole beans are what he usually mentions first. They were cooked in their pods and finished with hunks of bacon that Aunt Mae cured herself, along with country ham my dad claims was less salty and more delectably porky than any other he's tried. Fried chicken. Roast chicken, too, with a dressing full of homemade sausage. Big, fluffy biscuits smothered in white chicken gravy—or just a smear of Aunt Mae's sweet butter. Uncle Ed liked to pour Caro syrup over his plate, though Aunt Mae denounced it as low-class: 'You don't do that to good food!'

What good food is was precisely what young Fred was absorbing at Aunt Mae's table. That, and a sense of how, when something is made with care, you appreciate it with equal care; how food can be a way for people who aren't otherwise especially demonstrative to express themselves.

It's not a lesson he would have learned at his mother's table—or not in the same way. My grandmother had little use for cooking. Born on a farm not far from where Aunt Mae and Uncle Ed's place was, she'd escaped to Louisville and nursing school and kicked up her heels just as soon as her parents blinked. (I remember her saying once, deadly serious, 'It didn't matter who I went out with. I was not staying home on a Saturday night!') Her given name was Mary Willie—on her wedding day she became, improbably, Mary Willie McCracken Kracklauer—but everybody called her Billie. She called everybody sug, as in sugar, as in, 'Listen, sug, could you get me another Manhattan?'

By the time I was born, Grandpa Kracklauer had long

since died, and Grandma was back in Louisville. Each summer, like a salmon finding its way upstream to its spawning place, my father packed us in the station wagon for the trip to Kentucky. On the way down the Dixie Highway, he'd call out various landmarks—our favorite being the auto-wrecking yard near Fort Knox that was featured in the movie Goldfinger (the scene where Oddjob kills the guy in his car and then has both car and body crushed in a compactor). At Grandma's apartment, we'd sit at the kitchen table while she smoked Parliament cigarette after Parliament cigarette and held court with whichever relatives had stopped in because Fred and his family were in town.

With her husky voice and commanding presence, Grandma was, to me, like a Louisvillian Lauren Bacall. Enveloped in her particular atmosphere, suffused with tobacco and the jasmine lilt of Blue Grass by Elizabeth Arden, you knew you were where the action was. An unrepentant hedonist—my father is definitely her son in this regard, and I his daughter—she loved eating and drinking, and most of all doing those things out in the world, in restaurants, of which Louisville has always had many good ones. But the salient meals of our annual trip happened outside the city.

We'd go out and visit Aunt Mae and Uncle Ed and their three-legged dog, Tippy—that is, until Tippy met his end, heroically, seizing and killing a rabid fox that charged Aunt Mae while she was hanging laundry in the yard. (This story loomed large in our family mythology; back in Pittsburgh, our schnauzer was never called upon to rise to such an occasion.) There was a grape arbor outside the kitchen door, and a blackberry bramble along the fence. I remember Aunt Mae putting on her bonnet, gently leading me by the hand out to the bramble, and showing me how to pluck the squishy, dark fruit from the prickly branches. She baked her berries into juicy cobblers, and her cherries and peaches into pies with lattice tops. Like our father before us, my brother, sister and I happily ate it all up.

The culmination of every trip was a meal at the Doe Run Inn, in nearby Brandenburg. The restaurant was in an old stone mill built in the early nineteenth century by Squire Boone (brother of Daniel). It had a wide, breezy screened porch overlooking a small waterfall that kicked up a mist, making this possibly the coolest place in all of Kentucky on a hot afternoon. We'd sit at a long table on that porch with a rotating cast of aunts and uncles and cousins, and eat food jam-packed with a taste I guess I'd now call umami, but back then could only experience, not articulate. Ruddy, intensely salty shards of cured, aged country ham, for example: the savory flavor was so concentrated, and so addictive, I had to gulp down lemonade in order to keep eating it. Fried chicken livers with a breading as ethereal as tempura and a velvety interior that tasted like iron and earth. As a small kid, I preferred the fried chicken—crunchy and peppery outside, moist and silky within. Even the creamy salad dressing, dolloped on wedges of sweet iceberg lettuce, was powerfully flavorful, clotted with curds of pungent blue cheese. And then, for dessert, a slice of tart, gooey lemon chess pie.

There were dishes, I'll admit, that were too much for

my palate. The chicken livers at first (though I grew to love them later). And the ham balls: dense little depth-charges of minced country ham, fried until they were brown and caramelized on the outside, submerged in a sauce made from rendered ham fat and sweet, vegetal sorghum syrup. The ham balls overpowered me—flavors I loved, delivered at an intensity so fierce I couldn't handle it. But give me a pillowy baking-powder biscuit doused in gravy made with that same fat and syrup, and I was the happiest girl in the world. It was all about the ratio of lip-smacking, savory goodness to buttery, serotonin-spiking starch. These full-on flavors were making me sit up and notice what I liked and craved, and in what degrees. It shaped the way I came to assess all food, whether in Louisville, Pittsburgh, Guadalajara or Seoul.

As everyone ate, they talked about what they were eating— what the cooks must have done to make it so good, how it compared to the way Aunt Mae did it, or Aunt Anna, or the cooks who were in the Doe Run kitchen twenty years ago. The gravity they brought to the ritual held them together. This was what an intact family looked like. 'Don't you like the chicken livers?' someone would inevitably ask me. So I kept on eating them until I did.

⇥

Ten or fifteen summers ago, my family paid a visit to the Doe Run Inn and learned that it had changed hands. The menu now featured such dishes as salmon grilled on a cedar plank and chicken Caesar salad. We were horrified.

It wasn't long before cousin Jeanne took matters into her own hands. Jeanne works for the local telephone company and had often held work events at the Doe Run Inn. She tracked down the previous owners and got them to hand over their recipes. Then she marched over to the restaurant and said, 'Here. This is how it's done.' Jeanne's not the sort of lady you say no to.

And so the old favorites were restored—the chicken livers, the biscuits, the chess pie—but it was never quite the same. The topography around there isn't as we remember it, either. The landmarks have changed. Along the road leading up to Aunt Mae and Uncle Ed's, what was once farmland is now overlaid with a grid of semi-suburban development. Dad has a hard time finding his way.

Last summer, we arrived to find a sign tacked to the front of the Doe Run Inn: 'Closed until further notice.' When we asked what had happened, cousin Pat shook his head. 'You know, the last time I was there, the fried chicken was greasy. Greasy chicken at the Doe Run Inn. That was it. I knew I could never go back.'

Still, the annual barbecue carries on, migrating, along with the hulking smoker hiked up on rubber tires, between the cousins' houses. Dad takes his place among the dwindling group of his contemporaries. We make our way down the long tables of food, we pile our plates with juicy pulled pork, we defy the humidity with cold beers and hand-churned ice cream made with fresh-picked peaches. This, at least, is exactly as we remember it.

Regarded by many as the world authority on Indian food, **MADHUR JAFFREY** is an award-winning actress and bestselling cookery author. She has appeared in over 20 films and written numerous cookery books, including the seminal *An Invitation to Indian Cookery*, published in 1973.

CUISINE BY DESIGN

Madhur Jaffrey

The balmy, consoling air has been entirely shut out by my hired car's fierce air conditioning. We are driving up Sri Lanka's west coast on a road that slithers along sluggishly, hugging the shore. Palms lean forgivingly towards waters blasted recently by a cruel tsunami. Bananas and papayas continue to produce, beguiled by the smiling sun. Uniformed children, their dark hair gleaming with massages of coconut oil, walk to school, books and sometimes cricket bats in hand.

I am headed towards my final stop in the country, the town of Bentota, where Sri Lanka's renowned twentieth-century architect and designer, Geoffrey Bawa, had built, perhaps sculpted is a better word, his country house and garden, Lunuganga. I am going there for a reason.

After returning from my last trip to Sri Lanka I had found that the glorious foods I had eaten were seamlessly linked in my memory to the places where I had eaten them and that some of the best of these were boutique hotels in old colonial houses or newer houses, restaurants and hotels, redone or freshly built with such a sense of Sri Lankan style, such a unique feel of Bawa-influenced, timeless modernity as to remain unmatched in all of Asia, indeed in the world. The combination of food and setting had been idyllic, a paean to a single, '60s architect. No other country in the world pays obeisance to a single architect (and now his disciples) with offerings of the country's best food or, in other words, no country offers its best foods in halls influenced by the modernist thinking of a single designer.

I have traveled over much of the world and eaten some wonderful food in great-looking restaurants. It is only in Sri Lanka that one constantly senses the benign, cohesive presence of one single master, who, with his disciples, has set the tone for what temples of hospitality should look like—spare, well proportioned and as allied to nature as possible. One has only to look at his erstwhile Colombo office, with its sleek water tank in front, which has now been converted to one of the city's most popular restaurants, The Gallery Café on Paradise Road. It was handed over to chef and designer Shanth Fernando on the condition that he always display art. Today it houses a hot restaurant and a tiny shop selling some of Sri Lanka's most exquisite handicrafts (I buy dozens of rice straw tablemats here). Trendily dressed diners who seem to know each other table-hop from the first course to the last, creating the buzz of a successful party. You may dine on beef *smore*, the spicy, coconut-sauced pot roast, or on the more eclectic mullet served with a green papaya salad or the Dutch burgher dish of deep-fried eggplant batons dressed with vinegar and coconut palm sugar.

On this trip, I had started out in Colombo, in the home of Sunela Jayewardene, a post-Bawa architect but one not untouched by the prescient master's love of nature and ecologically informed design.

Sunela Jayewardene lives in a top corner of her mother's grand colonial house. Young and already renowned, she has taken advantage of its very high ceilings to fashion an airy nest of her own in its upper reaches—a private, flowing, modern, multi-leveled, adobe-walled apartment. The highest perch of all has been reserved for dining and it is here that we are seated around an ornate antique rosewood table enjoying breakfast.

We have already sipped our king coconut in the living room a few steps below. These large orange coconuts, sold at street corners, burst with nutrients. As my driver explained to me earlier, 'They are very healthy, madam. You could survive six months on just their juice. We never use them for cooking. The green ones are good enough for that.'

The filtered morning light dances, almost by design, on the bluish-purple water lilies, Sri Lanka's national flower, massed in the center of the table, as we are offered *kola kanda*, a national porridge. We ladle this into our nineteenth-century Dutch-trade bowls. The porridge, made of red-hulled rice, coconut milk and varying foraged herbs—here it is the crawling green, *iramusu*, 'good for the kidneys', as everyone agrees—is served with pieces of raw brown sugar (palm jaggery) which we are meant to suck on with each spoonful. It is addictively good.

The next course consists of glorious egg hoppers. Common to both the South Indian state of Kerala and to all of Sri Lanka, hoppers (*appa* in Sri Lanka, *appam* in India) are crisply filigree-edged but spongy-in-the-center, bowl-shaped (because they are made in small, high-sided woks), rice flour and coconut milk pancakes. With an egg dropped in the center, they become egg hoppers. This can be done with such perfect timing that soft, medium or well-done eggs may be requested. To accompany the hopper, and to give it its Sri Lankan edge, are two relishes: *seeni sambol*, made with caramelized onions and tomatoes, aromatic pandan leaf, smoked and dried 'Maldive' fish bits, cinnamon, sugar and chilies; and *kuni mallung*, a lightly cooked dish of tiny shrimp and freshly grated coconut.

When we have scraped the last traces of egg yolk off our plates, we are offered, among other things, string hoppers, *idi appa*, fresh rice flour noodles, which appear as little red nests, made with red-hulled rice dough squeezed out of molds and steamed. String hoppers are generally served with the scrumptious, slightly tart *kiri hodi*, a curry leaf and fenugreek flavored coconut sauce, but here potatoes have been added to it to make a more substantial variation, *ala hodi*.

In these few dishes are many of the salient features of Sri Lanka's way of eating. The population (and main religion, Buddhism) of this tropical island nation came mainly from India some millennia ago, bringing with it a tradition of herbal remedies incorporated into everyday foods. As only a narrow channel of water separates Sri Lanka from south-eastern India, its cuisine shares many recipes and traditions with the Indian states closest to it, Tamil Nadu and Kerala, and rice remains the heart of the meal.

But while Sri Lanka stretches out one hand to India, it stretches out the other to Indonesia and Malaysia, with which it has primeval links. Hence the aromatic seasonings that lend a special *je ne sais quoi* to its cuisine include pandan leaves, lemongrass and the beloved dried 'Maldive' fish, *umbalakada*.

'Maldive' fish is dried bonito. It dries as hard as wood and is lovingly used in some form all along the arc that stretches from Japan to the Maldives. Small, kindling-like pieces, pounded before use, become the black gold that give Sri Lankan sambols and sauces their gloriously dark, smoky base notes. The Sri Lankans once bought theirs from neighboring Maldivians—hence the name—but now the curing is done in Sri Lanka.

Adding a different slant to Sri Lanka's cuisines are the influences of its early traders and settlers, the Arabs for one, who added basmati rice biriyanis and tripe curries to its culinary repertoire. Then came a succession of partial and total Western colonizers, the Portuguese, the Dutch, and finally, the British, whose combined cuisine—with Dutch influence predominating and Sri Lankan spices playing a provocative role—is known as Burgher food. The most famous Burgher may well be the deceased, mixed-race Bawa himself and the most famous Burgher dish might be *lampries*.

I attend a Burgher ladies lunch at the dazzling, modern
Colombo home of Anitra Pieris, whose family introduced
the now ubiquitous *Bajaj*, a motorized, three-wheeled
rickshaw, to the country. As Sri Lankan beauties gather and
gossip, ginger beer—a cooling, restorative drink of lemon-
grass-flavored syrup mixed with ginger and lime juice—is
served. Lunch starts with the pièce de résistance, *lampries*,
from the Dutch word *lomprijst* or 'a packet of rice'. A banana
leaf–wrapped package of food based on the traditional Sri
Lankan meal of rice and curry with hints of Indonesia, where
the Dutch had also ruled, this is so loved that it is frequently
frozen and sent to relatives around the world.

I open my baked packet. There is the rice, perfumed with
cardamom, cloves and pandan leaves and cooked in stock.
There is a dryish, tamarind-tart and chili-hot curry made
with diced pork, beef and chicken. There are *frikkadels*, beef
meatballs, a sweet, hot and sour eggplant and green pepper
pahe, the *seeni sambol* made with shallots, and a marble-sized
ball of *blachang*, very similar to the *belacans* of Indonesia and
Thailand but here made at home with pounded dried shrimp,
garlic, ginger, chilies, sugar and lime juice. Even the gods in
the heavens must love *lampries*. I barely have room left for
the beef smore, a curried pot roast soured with lime pickle
or, indeed, the cashew-dotted semolina love cake with its
haunting smell of nutmeg.

For most Sri Lankans, meals generally consist of a simpler
'rice and curry'. Where is a traveler to find the very best? I
am told to head straight to Ena de Silva's house in Matale,
just outside Kandy. Ena is among the last surviving members

of the Bawa pack. A stunning beauty in her time, she did all the large batiks that decorated Bawa's buildings. She serves lunches upon request only. They must be ordered at least a week in advance.

A stop for dinner and sleep along the way at Kandy House in Kandy is suggested. Kandy is in the cooler hills, an ancient city built around a lake where the British deposed the last Kandyan king and took power in 1815. In 2005 Kandy House, a two-hundred-year-old mansion, was magically transformed into a gleaming, spare boutique hotel by Channa Daswatte, a disciple of Bawa and now a renowned architect himself. As I enter I notice two long Ena de Silva batiks displayed like banners. The superb, free-form, modernist food here, served on a back verandah overlooking a lush garden and prepared with fresh, local ingredients, could include goat brain on toast with ash gourd sambol or ravioli filled with jackfruit seeds and water spinach. For breakfast, fresh hoppers are always available.

At Kandy House, they know the short cut to Ena De Silva's residence in Matale, north of Kandy, useful information as Ena expects you on time. Matale, still in the hills, is the center of the spice trade. There are spice gardens all along the road eager to show visitors their wealth of black pepper vines, nutmeg, clove and cinnamon trees. It was the cinnamon— and gems like rubies—that drew the early traders, the Phoenicians and the Arabs, and then the Europeans here in the first place.

A sign for the Ena's Uluwihare Kitchen points uphill. We leave the main road, winding our way up to a private estate.

A long stone house sits on a ledge overlooking the valley and the Kandyan hills beyond. I am seated in the narrow front patio, admiring the eastern view, when Ena appears, a theatrical vision in three hats, one on top of the other, yellow walking stick, shiny sneakers, sparkling lips and a sequined, jeweled jeans outfit worthy of Elvis. She is a woman of style. Her own style. She was eighty-four at the time.

With a heart and talent larger than life, the Ena de Silva style starts with herself, goes on to her patio, over-laden with garden bric-a-brac, enters her living-dining room, bedrooms and bathrooms, where every surface is covered with patterns and cloths and where valuable ebony and mahogany furniture holds equal place with paper flowers, brightly painted chairs and an eclectic collection of tchotchkes. It even goes into her small, sooty kitchen, where the walls are painted with primitive figures. Her style might be considered anti-Bawa Bawa-ist, very personal and anti-elitist.

The kitchen is sooty for good reason. The mouth-watering food that it sends forth is all cooked over wood, as that is deemed the best fuel. At her rice and curry lunch there are at least twenty dishes, some laid out on trolleys and side tables, others served directly by Ena's manservant. The rice, as she is entertaining, is green coriander rice, a basmati perfumed with garlic, ginger, lemongrass, pandanus leaves and, of course, lots of green coriander. There is a most delicious red chicken curry for which skinned chicken pieces are marinated overnight in very red chili powder, curry powder, turmeric, vinegar, salt and shallots. The next day, they are cooked with more shallots, garlic, fenugreek, lemongrass, pandan, curry leaves and coconut milk. The tuna curry has hints of cardamom, cinnamon and lemongrass; there is a dal curry made with whole roasted and pounded mung beans and coconut milk; a ridge gourd curry; a carrot, cashew and pea curry; a pumpkin and long bean curry; and an okra curry.

Then, there are all the side dishes needed to complete the meal. The barely cooked *mallungs* are unique to Sri Lanka. There are two here: for the exquisite tuna and snake gourd *mallung*, tuna is lightly poached first and shredded. Then a little oil is heated in a pan, a few mustard seeds are allowed to pop in it and the tuna as well as finely diced gourd, grated coconut and green chilies are all packed down and allowed to steam in their own juices for a few minutes. Fresh lime juice is squeezed in at the end. A second *mallung* is made with thin shreds of a quick-wilted, collard-like green. It is worth the price of a Broadway show just to watch the art of speed-shredding a basketful of greens into hair-thin shreds with a kitchen knife.

Other side dishes offer crunch and spice—fried bitter gourd slices, fried dried Bombay Duck (a fish) and many fiery relishes, the sambols, one made with okra and shallots and the most popular everyday *pol sambol*, made with grated coconut, crushed red chilies, shallots and lime juice. We end with rich water-buffalo yogurt served with *kitul* palm honey.

I go south from Matale, heading towards the mountainous Tea Trails to stay on a tea plantation. As the drive is long, I stop for a roadside break of tea and 'Chinese' rolls (fish spiced with green chilies and curry leaves, wrapped in a pancake and deep-fried). I also enjoy an equally spicy fish bun and a scrumptious *malu cutliss*, a spiced fish ball, sometimes served with drinks, belonging to a family of foods that Sri Lankans lovingly call 'short eats'.

At Nuwara Eliya, 6000 feet above sea level, there are tea plantations as far as the eye can see, neat green mounds on hillsides, poised for a Seurat to paint them. The tea trees have all been kept trimmed as table-top dwarfs for easy picking of the required 'two leaves and a bud'. This is such a labor-intensive process that Sir Arthur C. Clark, who lived in Sri Lanka, wondered if the tea industry could last much longer. Once this area was home to Sri Lanka's richest forests, filled with wild bears, leopards and elephants. The forests were cleared at great cost and now Sri Lanka produces, in all, about 700 million pounds of tea annually. The tea planters led luxurious but somewhat lonely lives and now many of their homes have been converted into small hotels.

Castlereigh, on a hill overlooking a reservoir, is one of them. I might as well be in Britain. It is cool, I am surrounded by an English garden and at 5pm there are undistinguished scones and jam for tea. But you can ask for Sri Lankan food at every meal and it is far, far better.

I then head to the south coast, to Galle (pronounced Gaul), and its most idyllic section, the Galle Fort, which I just love. Once an important port where Solomon traded for jewels, peacocks and spices, this walled, colonial township was occupied by the Portuguese in the sixteenth century, the Dutch in the seventeenth and early eighteenth and then the British until Sri Lankan independence. UNESCO has declared it a World Heritage Site as the whole, mostly Dutch, town, with its ochre-washed homes and narrow lanes, has been preserved, not as a museum but as a living township with boutiques, antique shops, jewel shops and cafes in the smaller houses and modern hotels in the larger mansions.

I stop at my favorite hotel, the gracious, exquisitely renovated Galle Fort Hotel. My suite has a four-poster bed with a mosquito netting. The sheets, pillow, the light throw are all luxurious and beautiful. I just want to live here. My dinner on the verandah overlooking an inner garden courtyard and a cool pool is a lazy rice and curry tiffin: a tuna fish curry *malu ambullthiyal*, soured with *goraka*, a smoked fruit skin, a *kukulmas* (chicken) curry flavored with the three fresh aromatics of this land—curry leaves, pandanus leaves and lemongrass—rice, and a salad-like sambol of fried bitter gourd, shallot slivers, tomatoes, chilies, lime juice and pounded Maldive fish. I eat, savor and melt into the warm night.

It is time to leave Galle and start on the coastal road north to my final destination, Bentota. A sign behind a closed gate, barely visible for the tropical greenery leaning over it, reads: LUNUGANGA, The Country Estate of Geoffrey Bawa, Private Property. I have come to pay homage at the shrine, now a part-time boutique hotel where meals may be ordered in advance.

This was a cinnamon plantation once, then a rubber estate when Bawa took it over, with a small unprepossessing house on a rise. Bawa proceeded to transform it and the land it was on.

Bawa spent most of his time on the back verandah, overlooking a terraced garden and Dedduwa Lake beyond.

His guests today do the same. We sit just where he sat, eating our meals and looking at the views he created, every one of them sculpted to his design. We view the water through a strangely languorous frangipani tree on whose growing boughs he hung weights to induce the curves he desired. Here we lunch on the exotic offerings from the kitchen: shredded raw pumpkin salad with grated coconut, shallots, chilies and lime juice, and a superb, mustard seed-flecked dish of sautéed, crisp, wing beans.

Today, among Sri Lanka's cognoscenti, design and food are a fixation, part of their modern being. Geoffrey Bawa's spirit must be so pleased.

TOM CARSON is the author of *Gilligan's Wake* and *Daisy Buchanan's Daughter*. A two-time winner of the National Magazine Award for criticism, he is currently *GQ*'s movie reviewer and a regular contributor to *The American Prospect*.

A WEDDING FEAST

Tom Carson

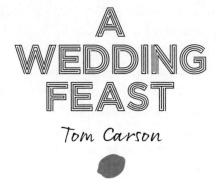

My mother can't stand cilantro. The cooking gods wrathfully sent her on State Department postings to India and Mexico to cure that blight, but they didn't know Mom. She outfoxed them by taking no interest in the local cuisine. That stayed true in every foreign country where she put in time on the taxpayers' tab.

New Delhi was her first post as a junior consular officer when she went into the family business. My father, whose own assignments had taken us in my Wonder Years to West Africa and then Germany, fell ill soon after arriving in Haiti as our embassy's new No. 2. Medevacked first to Gitmo—not then a byword for American disgrace, and at least he didn't live to see *that* crap—he was flown home to Bethesda Naval Hospital.

It was a fitting last stop on the big trolley for an Oregon lad who'd been a teenage sailor in World War II. My sisters and

I rolled all six of our eyes when Mom—Mom!—took her first dogged steps toward behaving like the head of the family. Yet the Foreign Service took care of its own in those days, so Dad's pals pulled strings to get his widow into the lowly consular corps. They never guessed her career would last longer and be more distinguished than his.

In most ways, my eager mother was open enough to whatever India had on tap to rate as unconventional. She cultivated oodles of Indian friends—not just for work, but because she *enjoyed* them—and preferred an apartment in unfashionable Greater Kailash to the American compound. Her gig also took her to nooks of India few diplomats saw, including its jails.

But the food? Not a chance. I was in college back then, meaning our government paid for me to come to Delhi every Christmas. My mother had a good cook named Joseph, who was more or less resigned to wrangling menus that wouldn't have looked exotic at an Applebee's in Des Moines. I still remember when she announced that, as a special treat—for him, I think, not us—Joseph was going to prepare us our one Indian meal.

One. He waved me afterward into the kitchen to taste the version he'd cooked up on the side for himself. How he relished my discovery that the stuff he'd served us was as bland as baby food by comparison.

And *plus ça change*, and so on, Dad. There may be Foreign Service families whose members delight in expertly whipping up the tagines they learned to love in Morocco, but we were never one of those. My kid sis and I once amused ourselves by concocting a guide to the real—and fondly remembered—ethnic cuisine of our childhoods: airline food.

Since there were usually 7-11s nearby in my bachelor years, I didn't learn to cook or own a single cookbook until I got married at age thirty-two. The big exception—my showcase dish—was fettucine Alfredo, a recipe Forrest Gump could cope with: buttload of cheese, buttload of cream, mix with pasta. Add pepper and nutmeg, and I might get laid.

After I'd proudly made it five or six times, my wife begged me to stop. Wasn't I getting laid anyway? And—more important—did I want to put that status at risk? If that cholesterol ziggurat were put in front of me today, I'd throw up. If I ever put it in front of her, I'd be wearing a dripping saucepan, like, *instanter*.

Marriage had also introduced me to a culinary mentor: my new mother-in-law. Raised rural in British Columbia until she headed south as a bride, she'd long since been cosmopolized by Los Angeles, America's most cosmopolitan city. Her fluency in half a dozen cuisines—India's more than most, since my wife's stepdad, Om, hailed from there—wasn't the only proof.

Not least because it was far from her only skill, Maggie made a life bereft of cooking's pleasures seem forlorn. Even more than the outcomes, I was smitten by how she went about it: the alternating rhythms of patience and dispatch, the trick bag of adaptable techniques, the logistics of a complicated *mise en place*. I'd just never understood how simply, nihilism-defyingly happy you could make other people by cooking well.

It also reminded me of a trade I did know by then. How can any writer *not* love to cook? Maggie, who writes pretty good poetry, will be baffled to learn how often I mentally murmured Michael Corleone's line in *The Godfather, Part II*: 'You're a great man, Mr. Roth. I have much to learn from you.'

Since she also thought no married couple should settle for call-it-macaroni, cookbooks became our staple gifts. She started us off with baby steps: Jeff Smith's Frugal Gourmet books, still a gateway drug I'd recommend even if the late Jeff proved to be no wonderful role model as a human being. But soon came the first curveball: Tommy Tang's *Modern Thai Cuisine,* emphasis on the 'modern'.

Tommy was in vogue then. My fellow LA transplant's signature restaurant was on Melrose Avenue, which may say it all. Even I could guess that dishes this heavy on pine nuts, cream and other Western ingredients weren't Thai food as it was eaten in Bangkok. Tommy might have *liked* my fettucine Alfredo.

It didn't matter. An Asian grocery the size and intricacy of a nuclear submarine was just across Sunset Boulevard from our home. Curry pastes, chili sauce, tamarind—how I loved and still love to soak tamarind for *meekrob*, rubbing the meat from the seeds in ever darker water before straining the juice—were all at my fingertips.

Within months, I'd floored an intern at the alt-weekly where my wife and I worked by declaring that I'd rather meet Tommy Tang than Mick Jagger. That may have been around when my indignantly pro-Anita piece on the Anita

Hill/Clarence Thomas Supreme Court hearings won me
an admiring letter from Riane Eisler, one of the greatest
compliments of my life.

I never met Mick, let alone Riane. But I did meet Tommy,
sort of. He did a cooking class at Pasadena's swankiest
supermarket, and that's why our copy of *Modern Thai
Cuisine* is signed. I remember him marveling at how many
pages were already loose and tamarind-stained. '*For Tom and
Arion Hope you'll enjoy to use it at all times have fun TT,*' the
inscription reads, making me suspect he'd had some help
with the book's text. But he did spell my wife's name right, so
bless him. I cook from it to this day.

But Tommy too was a gateway drug compared to two
books Maggie gave me later. One was Carol Field's *The
Italian Baker,* and my Kalamata olive-studded *pane* Pugliese
is pretty fucking fierce. The other was Julie Sahni's *Classic
Indian Cooking,* your cue to start humming 'Tara's Theme'
from *Gone With the Wind.*

Julie, light of my life, fire of my stove. I'll never get great,
Joseph—not like you—but I'm not bad. Maggie herself has
praised my *Shahi Murgh Badaami,* aka 'Royal Chicken in
Silky White Almond Sauce'. Since my mother-in-law doesn't
do unkindness, take that with a grain of Ms. Sahni's beloved
Kosher salt. I still regret that I never worked up the nerve to
make it for Om.

Can you appreciate the preposterousness? Unlike most of
my co-citizens, I'd *been* to India. I could have gorged on this

food three Uncle Sam–paid Christmases running, giving me a pseudo-connoisseur's head start. Why hadn't I asked Joseph about the spicings in his biryani? Had college-age me even known it was *called* biryani?

It was like learning that you'd spent adolescence surrounded by beautiful girls who really and truly wanted to sleep with you. But there you were playing chess or whatever.

Long gone from Los Angeles by 1997, my wife and I were living in the suburbs of Washington, D.C., and feeling grateful for superpower backwash. Vietnamese, Thai and Salvadoran restaurants were plentiful in neighborhoods I remembered as whiter than Justin Bieber in my Nixon-era high-school diaspora there. Then Maggie called to say that Om's niece Maneesha was getting married in Bhopal. And we were all going.

India! I hadn't been back in twenty-odd years. Plus, I now had a good bead on what to order for dinner. I could return with a newly swaggering sense of what India was all about.

Because I was and am foolish, I'd forgotten that India is always an argument, never a settled thing. And that no other country does either settled things or arguments better.

That disconnect first cropped up when I faced my father-in-law over menus soon after we landed. Hearing me wonder aloud about the restaurant's lamb korma—I'd made it so many times, and I wanted to learn how my version compared to the Olympics—Om politely typed 'No' with two fingers. I hadn't even noticed the tabletop included an invisible Smith-Corona.

234

'I don't trust meat in India,' he said, and that was the law from then on. While Om was the least despotic of men, I'd better explain that he was not only a doctor but a renowned one. There may be English majors who envy me because I once got to interview Kurt Vonnegut, and I don't blame 'em. They've got nothing on the way specialists in pulmonary diseases react when I mention that I was Om P. Sharma's son-in-law.

The reason I never disputed him in twenty-three years is that I'm a uniquely informed judge of my own poor character. I don't quarrel with people whose stellar one leaves me hungering for their good will.

Until now, though, I'd never seen Om in his Indian role as the family success story and New World dispenser of gifts. If I'd ever speculated that my mild father-in-law might have made an uncommonly thoughtful king—and I may have, since I loved him like an inadequate but loyal knight of Maggie's samosa-crammed round table—then Bhopal made that image no longer hypothetical.

Though sleeping elsewhere, we spent the three days leading up to the wedding in his sister Ansuiya's small house. As Om greeted delegations of relatives, his octogenarian mother monitored each reunion like a hummocky, misleadingly crumbled-looking fortress. Its main artillery—her eyes—had never run short of ammunition. I still remember how Maggie had to coach me with a murmured 'Now' to touch her feet in the traditional gesture of devotion.

The matriarch's role was to prevent me when I tried, and I've never been crazy about that kind of ritual. I'm American enough that self-abasement strikes me as a ceremony best

235

conducted in private. But the measure of how intimidating Om's mother was is that no one in the family has told me her name to this day. To imply she needed identifying would have been an insult. Because it would have been trivial, nobody told her mine either.

Her main concern, however, was to keep tabs on the procession of solemn female relatives fetching wonderful food until we men lolled about like gorged ticks. Me far more than Om, since he had family politics to negotiate whose cheerfulness-masked complexity might have worn out Richelieu. But while my wife and Maggie kept departing because they'd been included in one or another ceremony preparing Maneesha for her great day, my only job was to be fed to the gills as Om reduced big clouds to small talk.

As his son-in-law, I was automatically part of the settled thing, not the argument. I've never been such a *conscious* beneficiary of sexism in my life, and Riane Eisler's letter praising 'Something About Anita' was still warm. But in India, you learn as nowhere else that great cooking can be a source of pride because it began as a gesture of fealty.

Out of the blue, the France-born and noxious tradition of keeping certifiable great chefs male to identify the endeavor's importance began to look like one of patriarchy's more desperate fibs. After Bhopal, I had no trouble understanding why Indian cuisine's pioneer popularizers in the West—my beloved Julie, Madhur Jaffrey, even, for Christ's sake, Padma Lakshmi—have all been women. India recognizes their skills as part of the settled thing, and you grab leverage to become part of the argument where you can.

Before we eat, may I say that Om himself had major credentials as a male feminist. One of his foremost mentors had been a woman: Sheila Sherlock, M.D., whose biography he lovingly wrote not long before he died. The women he tutored to begin their own distinguished medical careers are legion. Lots of them spoke and some wept at his multiple memorials. Attending those kept my wife and Maggie boarding planes for several months in late 2012.

Yet Om had tersely expressed his major disagreements with his home country by decamping. Now that he was back, it would have been ridiculous to reproach how the settled things worked by voicing an argument.

What did those hushed women bring? Oh my god. Wonderful *palak paneer* (just spinach and cheese, but a dish whose delicacy had defeated my lone stab at it back in Arlington). *Aloo gobi*, which I'd never even tried to cook. *Ras malai*, aka sweet paneer dumplings in milk sauce. *Jalebis*, the perfect combination of pretzels and onion rings for those who fantasize about tasting both soaked in syrup by way of being greeted in heaven.

Keep in mind that all this was Bhopal's equivalent of one polite bowl of trail mix and a perfunctory bag of Doritos during the Super Bowl's pregame show. Maneesha and her bridegroom Vijay's wedding feast would be when the *real* food came out. Since I'm aware of the limits of my powers of description, I'll refer you to Keats on Chapman's Homer for the *bhindi masala* and *kali dal*—and, oh, biryani—once they plighted their troth.

How obsessed I got with the unseen, humidly fragrant kitchen from which all this was gravely emerging. I once worked up the nerve to ask Maggie if there was any chance they'd let me go back there to watch for a while. Knowing India better than I did, my mother-in-law looked at me with eyes round with horror. It took her a few seconds to muster a tactful way to tell me I'd be embarrassing and humiliating our cooks if she even relayed the request, since they might feel they had no choice but to accede to Om's bizarre American son-in-law and it would be a scandal. After that, I just shut up and ate my jalebis … like a good boy.

Maggie was wearing a sari at the time. So was my wife, to whom I think it meant more. (It wasn't her mom's debut in that outfit.) When our plane out of Bhopal got delayed, my wife burst into tears and stretched out on the floor, her head instantly pillowed by one of Om's female cousins who kept stroking her hair as she wept. Realizing that her consoler—who didn't speak English—might mistake her unhappiness for frustration, she kept stabbing the rug with her finger: 'I want to stay here. I want to *stay here.*'

My beloved, accomplished, thoroughly post-feminist wife and I have never spoken of that afternoon. I can't say whether we're shy about bringing it up or else we just both know.

Then came the miracle we still can't account for. (I literally just walked into the next room to ask her, and we swapped blank looks before we got back *au boulot.*) Reaching the airport, we learned the plane had been delayed yet again—and keep in mind, this was long before cell phones. But Om's sister Ansuiya showed up in the waiting lounge with tiffin. Hearing (but how?) that we were still in Bhopal, this woman past sixty had commanded her future son-in-law, Bunty, to

238

plant her on the back of his much-prized scooter. They rode to the airport through heavy traffic so she could bring us more food.

Once we got back to Arlington, my wife signed up to study Hindi for a couple of years and got pretty good at it. As for me, I went on cooking Julie Sahni's recipes—Madhur's, too? Madhur's, too—and I still sometimes do now. But with a new timorousness inhibiting my enthusiasm, for I have a better idea of what they mean.

Whether I love what they mean or feel dubious about the side dishes now comes in second to knowing I'll never be *part of it*. When you're a Foreign Service brat, you know at some level you'll never be part of anything. But we all have our fleeting, beautiful moments of hope, and my *rogan josh*—yes, I do trust meat here in America—is acceptable.

Maneesha and her husband Vijay are doing well. Om died last year in Los Angeles. I never knew what became of Joseph, and my 86-year-old mom still despises cilantro. As for my now widowed mother-in-law, who, like me, may now never see Bhopal again, Maggie came out in 2011 with a book of poetry called *Manjil*. I'd be lying if I didn't say that one of the poems in it I cherish most is the one she wrote about me in India.

CARLA HALL is a co-host of ABC's popular lifestyle series The Chew and is best known as a competitor on Bravo's Top Chef, where she won over audiences with her catch phrase "Hootie hoo" and her philosophy to always cook with love.

LEEK OF FAITH
Carla Hall

I grew up in Nashville, Tennessee, surrounded by the South's culinary heritage, but it took a trip to Paris to get me into the kitchen.

Today, I cook for a living, but for most of my life, I didn't know how to fry an egg. My grandmother on my mother's side was a good cook. My grandmother on my father's side was a good cook. My dad was a great cook. My mom? Well … three out of four ain't bad. My mom had no interest in cooking. It wasn't like she hated it. She just had no idea about it. She had gone away to boarding school at the age of twelve, and then went away for college, and had just never learned her way around the kitchen.

My dad could really cook, but my parents were divorced. Mom worked full time, and so, during the week, when my sister and I were in her care, we all happily lived off of frozen entrees, an occasional roast, and pancakes. On weekends, my father and grandparents would make collard greens, cornbread, smothered pork chops, fried catfish and mac and cheese, and more—food that then, and still today, is the ultimate comfort food for me. But like my mom, I had no interest in cooking the food. I was happy enough to eat it once it reached the table. Except for mastering an apple crisp when I was ten (it was a Girl Scout cooking badge requirement), I stayed pretty well clear of the kitchen.

When it came to college and my early working years, when circumstances forced me to cook now and again, the results were hit or miss. While sharing an apartment in college, my sister and I lived off of Chicken Divine (Kim's specialty, of baked chicken, broccoli and cheese thrown into jazzed-up cream of mushroom soup) and a passable spaghetti and red sauce (my signature dish; the sauce came out of a jar). If I strayed from the basics, disaster awaited. For my first job I moved to Tampa, Florida, where I worked as an accountant. I once tried to make vegetable soup for a couple of friends. I put four cans of tomato paste into the pot. When I served the meal, my friends gently asked if they could take me out for dinner.

It was a trip to Paris that set my life on a culinary course, but not for the usual reasons. I moved to Paris when I had had enough of accounting. I was twenty-three. I'd modeled in college, so I thought I'd give it a go full time, and I'd visited Paris once before, on an eighth-grade trip. Initially, I lived in a small hotel in the 14th arrondissement. It was a five-story walk-up. My room held a bed, a dresser, a sink,

and a small desk with a hot plate. The dormer ceiling kept
me from standing fully in some places. Though I was in the
gastronomic capital of Europe, you wouldn't have known
it from the way I ate. I dined on peas and tuna straight out
of the cans; muesli with powdered milk that I heated up
on the hot plate. When I needed groceries, I hit the small
convenience store next to the hotel.

It was the meals I had with my fellow models that changed
my life. When I arrived, I knew just one other person,
Rosalind Johnson, another African-American model. She
introduced me to her friends, and started inviting me to
Sunday brunches outside of Paris with her friends. It was
these brunches that opened my eyes to the power of cooking.

Rosalind's friends were also African-American, mostly
from New York and New Jersey. Though we were surrounded
by fantastic French food, everyone just wanted to cook dishes
from home—comforting, familiar dishes that I remembered
from weekends with my dad and grandparents. Mac and
cheese. Chicken wings. Pancakes. Eggs and sausages—all
kinds of things. They wanted to make turnip greens, they
said, but none of the French grocers sold them. I didn't even
consider helping—I saw my mother doing this whenever we
went somewhere, she would just watch. And so that's what I
did. I just hung out and watched and listened, astonished. It
was the first time I'd hung out in the kitchen while food was
being prepared, and I was enthralled. As the girls cooked,
they would say to one another, 'Oh, my mother does it like
this. My mother does it like that.' I had nothing to offer. I
realized that I had no idea what my grandmother did, or

what my father did. And I realized for the first time what I'd been missing all those years, and I was determined to make up for it.

Over the next several years, I shuttled between Paris and New York City, with an occasional boyfriend-visit to Washington, DC—I was in Paris when the fashion industry needed runway models, in the fall and spring, and would head to New York for its season to live with friends whenever my three-month visa ran out. Wherever I was, I cooked. I bought and read cookbooks. I read every food magazine I could get my hands on. But, remembering my canned tomato-paste soup fiasco, I didn't dare venture off the path each recipe set forth. I didn't trust that I would find my way back should I so much as inch a toe off the road.

I eventually left the small hotel and moved in with a friend, Patrice, who shared a flat with her French boyfriend. I slept on the couch. And I decided I would pay my way by cooking. I was excited, and eager to recreate and share the warmth that I had been experiencing at the Sunday brunches. I would make chicken pot pie.

I grew up loving chicken pot pie in its frozen form. And just once, to impress my boyfriend back in Washington DC, I'd made a pretty good version mostly from scratch, filling a store-bought pie crust with chicken and vegetables in a white roux, following the recipe instructions to the letter.

So off I went to the market, a small neighborhood store, recipe in hand. I needed chicken, onions, carrots, celery, mushrooms, flour, butter, stock, herbs and heavy cream. I found everything but the celery, which, comb the aisles as

I may, was nowhere to be found. Instead, I puzzled over a vegetable labeled *poireau*, which I later learned was a leek. At the time, I had no idea what it was. Only a crazy person would confuse it with celery but the colors were somewhat similar—the light green part of it, anyway—and its shape was similarly long and spear-like. And since celery itself was nowhere to be found, I grabbed a poireau and called it good.

Back at the flat and still filled with excitement, I started to get my ingredients together. I was acutely aware of the leek's wildcard nature. I stared at it from different angles. I smelled it. I twirled it like a baton. Finally, I tasted a small, raw piece of it. It tasted like an onion, but milder, with onion-like layers. Ah! I thought. Could it be an overgrown scallion? I decided to treat it as such. I cut the root end off, cut the leek in half crosswise, and put it into the pot.

When it was finished, the pot pie filling was not what I expected. It was sweeter than usual. The dark green parts of the leek that I'd used were tough and slightly bitter. It was missing a tang, a zip. Was this the taste that the celery would have given it? Who knew? Celery was such an ordinary vegetable. One that didn't usually stand up and shout, 'I'm here'. But its absence was so loud that I couldn't hear anything else. The symphony of flavors that I had wanted to share was nowhere to be found. My friends loved it, but I knew it could have been better. I was profoundly disappointed.

But that failed pot pie transformed the way I thought about cooking. I had always loved puzzles as a child, and now I started to see recipes in a new light—not as rigid steps to

be followed, but as collections of separate pieces that could
be combined in different ways to make different, delicious
wholes. Eating out also became sort of a game of re-creation,
and I would try to figure out the ingredients and amounts in
a dish, whether at a restaurant or someone's house.

This new awareness of the elements of cooking changed
everything. Suddenly I was seeing the city in all of its
culinary richness—it was like going from black and white
to color when Dorothy leaves Kansas and touches down in
Oz. I was living on a budget, but each meal was a revelation.
The first time I ate a frisee salad with lardons and egg, I
loved how the frisee tickled my mouth, and marveled over
the savory nuggets of pork belly and the silken warmth of
the poached egg. I rhapsodized over a piece of pan-seared
fish in beurre blanc, so different from the fried catfish I
was used to. And I still vividly recall the blackberry pie
with a perfect crust served at a bookstore café. The simplest
things stood out in greater relief: the floral whiff of a grind
of cracked black pepper on a perfectly cooked steak (always
shared, of course, because I never had any money); the citric
zing a squeeze of lemon brought to a simple salad of mixed
greens.

This awareness, and interest, stayed with me. I carried
it from Paris to London (where I also modeled, and made
my first quiche, zucchini bread, and coronation chicken—
curry chicken salad with grapes and almonds—for my
appreciative roommates), and eventually back home to
the US, where I opened a catering business, and attended
culinary school, which has morphed into a career in food

media, cookbook writing, and more. Cooking is now my life, in ways I could have never anticipated or imagined.

As for leeks, after the pot pie, I avoided them for years, but they kept putting themselves in my hands. At my very first restaurant job, my task was to julienne leeks for sauces or rough chop them for stocks. At culinary school, we used them every which way. Today, I cherish them. I'll flour and fry them for a garnish for steaks. In the spring, when they are young, I braise them. They go into all of my sauces and all of my stews. I put them in tarts with mushrooms. I make a leek confit, cooking them slow and low until they turn into jam. And every time I go to look for them—looking for ones with a larger ratio of white to dark green, so I get my money's worth—it reminds me of how they set me on this path, which, like the leek itself, was so unexpected, so unlikely, and so very rewarding.

MA THANEGI is in her sixties and has lived in Yangon, Myanmar, since she was eight months old. She writes only on topics related to Myanmar, especially its people, because it annoys her no end that they were once ignored by the international media and are still largely misunderstood.

GUNS AND GLUTTONY ON THE CAMPAIGN TRAIL

Ma Thanegi

When Daw Aung San Suu Kyi, the daughter of our hero of independence General Aung San, emerged in August 1988 as the popular leader of the uprising for democracy, about thirty of us volunteered as her personal assistants and bodyguards. Most were students still in their teens with no training but acted as bodyguards in the literal sense because they only had their bodies to protect Ma Suu should she come under attack. The few adults were writers, poets, lawyers and artists, like me, who had set aside what we were doing to support her.

We were worried sick for the safety of Ma Suu (elder sister), or Aunty Suu as the students called her. In the state newspapers we often saw the ruling generals' speeches calling for the democratic opposition's 'annihilation'.

The student bodyguards felt they should be well prepared for any encounter with the annihilation process ... not to gather arms for protection but, like all good Buddhists, to gather merits for the next life and to ensure they departed with all requisite rituals completed. For that they joined the Buddhist order of monks and nuns for a week and had monks preside over the *tharanagone* ritual usually reserved for the dead. They cheerfully explained that they needed all the merits they could get. As they could not know for sure if their parents would be able to retrieve their bodies if they were shot down, they said they needed the death ritual, even if they were jumping the gun, so to speak.

After her party, the National League for Democracy, was formed on 24 September 1988, with Ma Suu as General Secretary, we travelled all over the country with her on the campaign trails. She gave speeches to the thousands who turned up in support in every town or village we passed through and met with party members when we stopped overnight or at least for an hour or so. Sometimes we encountered soldiers pointing their rifles at us but all of us, including the local supporters, simply looked at them with scornful expressions on our faces.

As the campaign wore on, day after day, all of us began to look dirtier and scragglier, tanned almost to the colour of tar and hollowed-eyed from exhaustion. While Ma Suu spoke to the crowds and the township supporters took over from us, we would scurry to find a space for a catnap. When the boys spotted something like a mat, however dirty or small, they would drop on it like a tangle of puppies and be snoring within seconds and I'd be curled up on my coat spread on the floor. But the meals lovingly prepared by Ma Suu's supporters made up for the exhaustion.

In the Buddhist culture of Myanmar, food is not only offered but thrust upon you. We'd often eat three lunches a day on the campaign trail, because in every town or village that Ma Suu visited, her supporters had already laid out a feast. After the second lunch Ma Suu, who ate like a dieting bird, would plead that she really couldn't accept anything more, but the villagers would pout and make muttered threats of war against the other towns that had fed us. So she would eat, just a little bit more.

We got so used to being fed at every place we stopped that once, at a whistle stop, a few of the boys marched into a yard set out with tables and plates of snacks, which they devoured. We found out only after we reached the next town that it was a private celebration being hosted by a member of the state-sponsored party, our biggest enemy. They had been furious but our supporters outnumbered theirs by thousands so they had said nothing. It was one of the many jokes our crowd shared.

Of all the meals we had, the most memorable was a dinner served by Buddhist nuns in a town near the coast called Mawlamyaing. Nuns in Myanmar follow the same monastic code as monks, fasting between noon and dawn the next day. The dinner was laid out in the traditional way, on several low, round tables in a large hall inside the nunnery; we sat on the floor, our bare feet carefully tucked away out of sight.

The tabletops were so covered with dishes that there was hardly room for our own plates. I remember one of the boys whispering to me about how bad he felt for the nuns who were serving us as they could handle and smell but not even taste the food. However, that guilty thought did not slow us down in stuffing our faces: the food was just too good.

We ate *hilsa* fish, which has a lovely deep flavour, and the nuns must have started work at dawn because this dish must be cooked for at least eight hours to soften its gazillion bones. There was butterfish, too, a cousin of the giant Mekong catfish. Its succulent flesh was perfectly set off by a thick gravy of pounded onions, garlic, ginger and crushed tomatoes. Huge prawns probably hauled from the Andaman Sea that morning, and nearly as big as lobsters, were bathed in a sauce of soft, sweet tomatoes enriched by the tomalley that had seeped from the crustaceans' heads.

To offset the creaminess there were plates of crisp-fried catfish and salted, dried snakehead fish that had been grilled, pounded until fluffy and drizzled with peanut oil.

There were sumptuous meats as well. I piled my plate with chunks of red-cooked pork, a dish from the central part of Myanmar. This, too, was a marvel of slow cooking: first the nuns had caramelised the sugar and quickly sautéed the large pieces of pork shoulder and finally simmered it for several hours until the rind was soft, the fat savoury, and the meat tender and flavourful. We were also served a curry of mutton and new potatoes laced with garam masala, and another curry of chicken. Beef is seldom served in Myanmar because the rice fields, source of sustenance for us, are tilled using cattle, and we owe a debt of gratitude to these benign creatures.

The richness of the meats and fishes was buoyed by the freshness of the salads, one made of blanched winged beans with tiny boiled shrimp, dressed with lime juice and pounded roasted peanuts. Another was raw prawn salad laced with lashings of kaffir lime juice and chopped green chillies. A third salad was a mixture of dried shrimp powder, fried onions, fish sauce and pennywort leaves, a plant recorded in our ancient medicinal texts as a cure for infections. There were vegetable dishes such as stir-fried water spinach with mushrooms, eggplant stewed with bits of pork belly, cauliflower fried with egg, and a thick vegetable stew with chickpeas, radish, okra, eggplant and squash made slightly tart with tamarind paste. Then, there was the dish never absent in Myanmar meals: a sour, spicy and salty relish to be eaten with chunks of blanched and raw vegetables. To cleanse our palates between mouthfuls there was a clear, piping hot fish soup seasoned with a sprinkling of tart roselle leaves. As is the custom in Myanmar, in lieu of dessert we ate *lahpet*, our national snack of pickled tea leaves served alongside fried beans, fried garlic, roasted sesame seeds, green chillies and nuts.

The meal lasted an hour and throughout it we remained silent, as Burmese etiquette demands, to show our respect for the food and for those who made it. This meal earned not only our respect, but our reverence.

⇾⊢

None of us were annihilated but we landed in Insein Prison in July 1989 while Ma Suu was placed under house arrest for the first of many times. For the first six months I endured the torment of not knowing if or when I'd be released until I said to myself, the hell with it, and stopped thinking about it.

Living conditions were primitive but there were no guards who tortured us. Although prisoners are allowed food parcels from home, we missed fresh cooked food and treats like ice cream. Each of us passed the prison years dreaming about food, talking about food and most of all licking our lips and laughing in memory of the feasts and fun we had on the campaign trail, never mind the guns.

SIGRID NUNEZ has published six novels, including *A Feather on the Breath of God*, *The Last of Her Kind*, and, most recently, *Salvation City*. She is also the author of *Sempre Susan: A Memoir of Susan Sontag*.

A TASTE OF COCONUT

Sigrid Nunez

I've eaten some of the best meals of my life in Paris, but when I think of that city the food that comes immediately to mind is a street vendor's chunks of fresh chilled coconut.

It was my first visit to Paris. I was twenty-one, just out of college, and traveling with a boyfriend. We'd taken the train from Frankfurt, which was where my sister then lived with her new husband, who was in the US Army and whom she'd married shortly before he was stationed in Germany. My mother was already visiting them when Stephan and I arrived, and for the next three weeks we tootled through parts of southern Germany, Austria and northern Italy, the five of us packed into my brother-in-law's Volkswagen Beetle. I confess this was one of the hardest things I've ever done.

We stopped for several days in my mother's hometown of Schwäbisch Gmünd, where her brother lived, and stayed with him in the same house where they'd both grown up and where I'd visited only once before, at the age of two. My sole memory of that first visit is of my grandmother locking me in a dark closet for calling her a witch. Whatever she may have thought, it wasn't name-calling; that severe woman terrified me. A wealth of family stories would later confirm that I was not far off the mark, and I can't say I entirely regretted not having had a second chance to meet Oma, who'd died suddenly the year before.

It was autumn. Without planning to, we hit Munich in the middle of Oktoberfest, where it seemed half the revellers were exuberantly sloshed Australians contending to drown out '*Bier hier! Bier hier!*' with 'More piss! More piss!' I've never been much of a beer-drinker, but I relished the traditional snacks, in particular my first taste of the large white German beer radishes, carved concertina-style and heavily salted—as I would relish my first ever gelato, made with real pistachio nuts and nothing like the artificially flavored psychedelic green ice cream back home, which was waiting for me in Bolzano. (So addictive was the flavor that, much later, living in Rome, I would eat pistachio gelato almost every day for a year.)

After we all returned to Frankfurt, Stephan and I continued on our way alone. Boarding the train for Paris, we neglected to bring any food. The train had no café car, we'd had nothing but coffee for breakfast, and as the hours passed we grew increasingly dismal. We kept lighting up in the vain hope that nicotine would take the edge off our hunger. To make matters more torturous, we were joined in our compartment by another American couple, who unpacked a picnic. 'You didn't bring food? Everyone knows you always bring food on European

trains,' the woman informed us. (And I can still see the brown
bread with its gleaming smear of butter topped by disks of pink
sausage in her hand; I can smell the bittersweet chocolate bars
that they broke out for dessert and ate with such infuriating
slowness.) *They* had been smart enough to bring lots of food—
none of which, however, they showed any inclination to share,
no matter how shamelessly I stared.

Lunch over, the woman settled back and made herself more
hateful by telling us what a miserable time lay in store for
anyone foolish enough to visit Paris without speaking good
French, which of course she did (allow her to demonstrate),
and we of course did not.

And so we arrived at the Gare de l'Est, famished and cranky
and tense with anxiety. In those days it was not uncommon
for American tourists to travel through Europe, even to major
cities, without bothering to book accommodations. You simply
headed for whatever quarter of Paris you wished to stay in,
equipped with a list of hotel names and the phrase *Avez-vous
une chambre pour la nuit*. This had worked flawlessly for
any number of people we knew, and we took the Métro to
Saint-Germain-des-Prés fully expecting it would work for us
too. (Having lived on a commune sometime earlier, Stephan
and I had had our fill of hippies and group lodging and were
determined on this trip to avoid youth hostels.)

Almost immediately we encountered two middle-aged
couples from Chicago who'd arrived an hour or so ahead of us
and who'd been running hither and thither in search of rooms.
They were having a tough time, one of the men said, because
'the girls' would not do without private baths.

Though we ourselves had no such requirement (in fact, we thought it absurd), our luck was no better. There were no vacancies at the hotels we tried. We stood helplessly with our bags in the Rue Bonaparte, feeling more like refugees than like a young couple on vacation. It was near sunset now and growing chilly, and I began to despair. The possibility of spending our first night in Paris without a roof over our heads seemed dismayingly real.

Even though I was the one who knew at least a little high school French and Stephan knew none at all, we agreed that he should continue the search alone while I waited with the bags.

I sank down onto one of the suitcases, feeling woefully conspicuous and worried that I might start sniffling. The past few weeks had had their share of trying moments. To begin with, hypersensitive to jet lag, I had not had a good night's sleep since leaving New York. Also, this happened to be a period when members of my family rarely saw eye to eye—or reason to be quiet about it—and every little disagreement had managed to blaze into a quarrel. And then, like most inexperienced tourists, we'd exhausted ourselves trying to do too much in the short time we had.

Yet even my misery couldn't blind me to the enchantments surrounding me. There is what filmmakers call the magic hour, and then there's the magic hour in Paris. And here came a quaint sight: a street sweeper, not a machine but a man using a handmade broom. As he passed he acknowledged me with a throaty 'mademoiselle' and touched his cap smartly.

'I may have found something,' Stephan said carefully. 'I'm not sure what you'll think, but just to prepare you, it's kind of a hole.'

A narrow old house in the Rue Jacob, dank and dark within. A strong odor of ammonia mixed with whatever the ammonia was meant to, but couldn't quite, get rid of. The room, up several flights of curving stairs (there was no elevator), was dingy and cramped and sinister looking. Had there been a rug, I would have looked for bloodstains on it. The iron bed was coated with rust, and the mattress was so curiously lumpy it might have been stuffed with dead cats. There was the smell of dead something, in any case. The only other furniture was a battered armoire (there was no closet) and a badly tattered armchair.

When we'd pictured ourselves going to bed in Paris, it was always somewhere modest, of course, but nevertheless, inevitably (it was Paris, after all) *charmant*. If the place had been merely austere, it wouldn't have been so bad. But this was seedy. I forbear to describe the state of the toilet. At least it was on the same floor; the shower, on the other hand (and there was only one), was way downstairs at the back of the ground floor. A crude structure with barely enough room to turn around, it was, as I recall, not entirely protected from the elements. Although, thank God, there was hot water, I couldn't imagine what it would've been like to shower in winter. A gap in one wall looked out on the backyard, turf to a couple of free-range (not that the term was in use back then) chickens.

We'd planned on having dinner in a restaurant that first night, but we were no longer up for it. We'd noticed several wonderful-looking food shops nearby, and we thought we'd buy a simple meal of bread and cheese to eat in our hotel room.

But this, too, turned out to be an ordeal, my bad French bewildering (but not amusing) shop servers and holding up other customers (it was the hour when these shops were at their busiest), whose intolerance I know I wasn't just imagining. I thought of the obnoxious sibyl on the train …

Back in the hotel, the only place to spread our supper was on the bed. We'd talked about going out after we finished eating, to a café, or at least for a walk, but instead we huddled in that glum little room, feeling fragile and incompetent and defeated.

An exquisite buttery croissant, a steaming bowl of café au lait—who doesn't know what's for breakfast in Paris, gourmet capital of the world?

We'd been told when we checked in that our tray would be waiting for us downstairs.

The dishes were cheap soft plastic, the coffee tasted insipid and was only lukewarm. No croissants, but four slices of inedibly stale American-style toast, a better use for which, as Stephan would later suggest to the front desk, might be shingling the roof.

We didn't know whether the grouchy old couple running the place were the proprietors or just caretakers. (I like to think that they not only owned the building but that they lived long enough to make a killing when properties in that quarter became among the costliest in the city.) It was he who prepared the breakfast trays and made the beds. More to our amusement than to our indignation, we noted that he was also hitting the Scotch bottle my brother-in-law had bought us in the Army PX and which we'd brought with us from Frankfurt. He spoke English quite well. He was not hostile like his wife, but he was not friendly either. With the black beret he wore even indoors, perched at an angle on his bristly white hair, and the frequency with which he expressed the Gallic shrug, he was the 'Frenchy' of old black-and-white Hollywood movies.

She spoke no English but managed perfectly to communicate the deep displeasure we gave her. It was she who was usually behind the front desk, and she scowled every time we passed as if she thought hotel guests were just about the worst idea anyone ever had.

The day before we left (our next stop was Amsterdam), we walked into an elegant *confiserie*, where I bought a bag of licorice drops. I'm a great lover of licorice—authentic, pungent licorice of the kind that's always been hard to find in the States. In Germany I'd discovered some excellent varieties, but this French licorice tasted evil to me. Stephan wanted none of it, either. But rather than throw the bag away, I thought of offering it to Madame when we checked out.

I was afraid she'd respond with her usual rancor. Instead she snatched the bag from my hand, crushed it to her chest, and thanked me with wide-eyed joy, like a child who hasn't seen candy in ages. It was good to have this for our last impression of her.

But wait. Here we are already leaving Paris and I haven't said anything about the coconut. Nor have I said that, despite the rocky start, we ended up having a fabulous time. Though lack of French continued to cause trouble—resulting, for example, in my once getting pâté when I thought I'd ordered soup and another time getting pasta when I thought I'd ordered pâté—clearly the woman on the train had been full of *merde*. (I've since met a couple who told of being outraged when the cashier in a Paris *supermarché* refused to ring up the tin of pâté they'd set on the counter with a baguette and some cheese and wine; only when he pointed at the tin and said meow did they understand.)

Now I can't say whether it was the Boulevard Saint-Germain or the Boulevard Saint-Michel where the street vendor had his stand, but it was a spot that we passed often during our ten days in Paris. The raw pieces, which cost a franc (twenty-five cents) apiece, were kept submerged in bowls of water. It did not occur to me then how unsanitary this was. But if you want to enjoy street food, you can't be too concerned about hygiene. Better to think what Orhan Pamuk writes (quoting a friend of his Istanbul childhood), that it's the dirt that gives it its flavor.

The vendor looked about my age, and though shabbily dressed had golden hair and noble features: both prince and pauper. I thought he might be one of the many students who filled that quarter. If so, he never went to class. All day and well into the night he was there with his bowls of coconut, and the same late October air that kept the pieces nicely chilled made him turn up his collar and bunch his hands inside his frayed pockets.

I had never eaten fresh coconut before and I found it delicious: just the right degree of sweetness and just the right coolness and size for a refreshing light snack. Whether hungry or not, I had to have a piece any time we happened to be near his stand. Though perhaps it was really him I craved. He had a sweet smile, his teeth as white as the coconut meat.

That's all. A small thing. A minor episode of my Parisian adventure. But such is memory that, ever after, it would not be the roasted squab (even better than the pigeon I knew from the

Chinese restaurants where my father worked as a waiter);
it would not be the snails, or the tournedos and mushroom
sauce; it would not be the *pommes frites*, or the *salade niçoise*,
or the lemon soufflé that lived on as the taste of Paris for me,
but the un-French coconut.

And now another gastronomic moment comes back—it,
too, a memory of street food.

Walking along the Seine one day, I had one of those bolts
of homesickness that can strike even in the midst of the
most exciting and enjoyable travels. And suddenly, more
than anything in the world, I wanted a hot dog. Luckily
we weren't far from the Eiffel Tower, where hot-dog carts
abounded. When I proposed to Stephan that we head there at
once, he stopped and stared at me. Back home in New York,
I never ate hot dogs. In fact, as he reminded me, I had always
expressed particular distaste, not to say disgust, for the idea
of eating any hot dog that came from a street cart. Which was
true. Still, I insisted. After all, we weren't back home, were
we. And once I had the thing in my hand I could not have
been happier. Indeed, that Paris hot dog survives as one of
the most powerful food memories of my life. I managed to eat
most of it before I started to cry.

There would be other trips to Paris (though never again
with Stephan: we broke up the following year). There would
be marvelous croissants for breakfast. Unforgettable meals
at places like L'Ami Louis and Jacques Cagna and Le Grand
Véfour. Nice hotels. *Reservations.* Paris for grown-ups, in
other words. Wonderful, wonderful, but there was a cost. The
cost was youth.

LOUISA ERMELINO is the reviews director of *Publishers Weekly* magazine and the author of three novels: *Joey Dee Gets Wise*, *The Black Madonna*, and *The Sisters Mallone*.

FISH HEADS

Louisa Ermelino

The hostel was dreary. Jakarta felt polluted, crowded and dirty after the island paradise of Bali, where we had rented a room in a family compound and discovered fruits worthy of fairy tales: mangos, mangosteens, jackfruit, papaya, and pale yellow pineapples cut into wedges. An enterprising young woman named Jenik had gotten herself a blender and access to electricity and, at a stand on the dirt road to Kuta Beach in 1968, the smoothie came to town. Jenik also figured out pancakes and French toast and would make omelettes with dirty blue-gray mushrooms … her eggs, your mushrooms … magic! But for how long can you watch the sunset and dance with the Barong? We had left home for adventure, to tip over the edge of comfort and familiarity, and Bali was only the first stop. We didn't have much of a plan, but we knew we were moving west, with India in our mind's eye, but far into the future. We had all the time in the world.

In Sydney we'd bought a series of tickets that would take us through Java and Sumatra to Singapore. We had bus tickets, ferry tickets, and chits that would get us lifts on trucks in Sumatra. We had small bags and bellies full of *nasi goreng* and chicken satay. We'd had a Christmas feast at a Chinese restaurant in Denpasar with turtle soup and a collection of lacquered birds that, if they had still had their feathers, would have done a taxidermy shop proud. We'd roasted goats on spits over wood fires on the beach and piglets in pits of charcoal. We were loving Indonesia. The dreary hostel and grimy city would be left behind as soon as we'd washed our clothes and changed some money.

The night before we were to leave Jakarta, a man came to the hostel dormitory. I don't remember if we thought it was odd that he was there, or how the conversation started, but he made us an offer that we thought we couldn't, and shouldn't, refuse. He convinced us that the overland trek to Singapore was a terrible undertaking. Unreliable transport, he said. Impenetrable jungle. Mosquitoes. Nowhere even remotely decent to eat or sleep. And it would take weeks. And it was the rainy season. What were we thinking? There were six of us. We looked at each other. What were we thinking? Of course, our new friend had the solution. A ship to Singapore. Ocean breezes, deck chairs, all meals included for the seven-day journey. I personally loved ships, loved being at sea, had sweet memories of crossing the Atlantic on the Italian line, coming to Australia on a freighter. Someone poked me. What would it cost? Important point. It sounded like a big-ticket item. We were backpackers, remember? someone said. Our new friend said not to worry. He would make it happen for us. He'd take our existing tickets plus a few extra rupiah. A bargain, he said.

We parted with our tickets and rupiah and the next morning we were at the dock, along with, it seemed, a thousand others—despite the appearance that the ship had no accommodations for passengers. It was outfitted for cargo, clearly. Pandemonium reigned. We made a quick decision to follow the crowd. We were the only foreigners but we were used to that, so we climbed the gangplank and got on board. Families were claiming spots, laying down mats. Space was tight because of the cargo, which appeared to be garbage, piled up high in the bow. There was also no way we were changing our minds and getting back off. The crowd was moving only one way. We spread out our sleeping bags and sat down on the deck. I had a flashback to summers in Coney Island, with beach blankets laid end to end held down by shoes and radios. The ship pulled out. Our fellow passengers started getting sick almost immediately. I closed my eyes and leaned against my backpack. Believe it or not, I was hungry.

I took good food for granted. I grew up a first generation Italian-American. We weren't big on ambiance (I don't think I saw a milk pitcher until I was of legal age) but we knew about food. Lamb at Easter, the rib chops as tiny as a baby's fist, the lamb's head, *capozelle*, split and roasted with parsley, garlic and parmigiano; minestrone soup with five kinds of fresh beans and gobs of pesto stirred in; veal shoulder stuffed with egg and bread and oregano. When I started traveling, I didn't know much about the world or what there was to see, but I was open to what there was to eat. Camembert in France, ham sandwiches with butter (butter? Hmmm), pork-liver pâté. In Italy, puntarella and buffalo mozzarella, sautéed rabbit, fresh figs. Yogurt and honey in Greece and feta with tomatoes and cucumbers; profiteroles, zaatar bread, King of Persia pistachios, roasted corn, duck eggs swallowed raw in a tea glass on the road overland to India.

A gong sounded. People started to stir, then slowly, stampede. A line formed that snaked the length of the ship. I didn't see any food. I didn't smell any food, but a gong and what could pass for a queue facing in one direction was enough for me. I imagined rice and vegetables with a fried egg on top, soup with scallions and cabbage and pillows of tofu, maybe a shred of pork or chicken. I hadn't eaten since early morning. The line moved but I was too far away to see anything. I smiled at the babies; I pushed with the best of them. I was very hungry and nearing my turn.

And soon, there in front of me were the servers, ladling food onto tin plates from two huge oil drums. I was pushed from behind, handed a tin plate, and pushed again.

I looked down. A ball of rice and two silvery fish heads. Maybe there were three. Fish heads? I liked the look of a whole fish on a plate as well as anyone: braised with ginger, or roasted with fennel. I even liked the way a whole fish looked after it was eaten. A charming head and tail and a beautiful skeleton of bones.

The rice was gummy, the fish heads were small, stuck in the rice, eyes staring. I didn't know what to do with them except look for a cat. My companions, English and Australian, gave back their plates and left the line empty-handed. They hadn't liked the Christmas turtle soup or the lacquered goose poised in flight. They pooled their money with a plan to bribe the crew. I decided not to give up. I was very hungry. I took my tin plate and went back to my place on the deck. I formed some rice into a ball with my fingers and shoveled it into my mouth with my thumb.

The fish heads looked at me. I picked one up and studied it. I poked at it with my fingers and found a small round of sweet white flesh at the cheek. And more to eat in the furrow at the top of the head, and above the eyes, at the forehead (if fish have a forehead). I broke it apart and sucked the bones. I ignored the eyes and the gelatinous bits (personal … aspic gives me shivers) and I started on the second head. I finished the rice. I rinsed my fingers and my plate. My travel friends, meanwhile, had managed to score a pineapple and a bag of mandarins for a small fortune. They set about rationing like shipwrecked sailors. I accepted a mandarin section. I have always liked fruit after a meal. I unzipped my sleeping bag and lay down on the deck. I dreamt of fish heads.

The next day lunch was fish heads and rice and dinner was fish heads and rice. Twice a day, every day, for seven days, I ate fish heads. I found more tasty bits. I found the joy in fish heads. I smiled at the babies. I breathed in the sea air.

The ship ultimately left us, not in Singapore, but on a tiny island off Malaysia that had never seen a tourist, where the police were kind enough to put us up in a jail cell for the night, and for another small fortune, we hired a boat to take us to Singapore. We went straight to Maxwell Road to eat amazing dishes at the open-air market: Hokkein mee (fried prawn noodles); Hainanese chicken rice; chili crab. I didn't miss the fish heads. But I've never forgotten them.

There was an old Italian man in my neighborhood who had served time in Alcatraz. In 'the hole', he said, they fed him bread and water. 'I'd put the bread aside,' he told me, 'and after two days it tasted like cake …' In Indonesia, I learned what he meant.

NEIL PERRY (AM) is one of Australia's leading and most influential chefs. He manages seven award-winning restaurants in Australia—Rockpool, Rockpool Bar & Grill Sydney, Melbourne and Perth, Spice Temple Sydney and Melbourne, and Rosetta Ristorante—and develops quarterly menus for Qantas' International First and Business Class travellers. He is also author of seven highly successful cookbooks and has a weekly food column in Fairfax's *Good Weekend* as well as a monthly column in *Qantas: The Australian Way*.

CITY OF WONDER

Neil Perry

I remember it like it was yesterday, driving into Paris from the airport. It was a beautiful May morning in 1984. This wasn't my first trip overseas. I had been to Athens seven years before, I just think it was the overwhelming beauty of everything I saw out the cab window and the fact that now, as a professional cook, I felt I was returning to where it all started; at that time, France was the undisputed king of gastronomy.

As we got closer and closer to Paris I simply couldn't believe the look, the vibe, the smell of the city. We drove down along the Seine and it called out to be investigated, but before we could do that we needed to get dropped at L'Hotel on the Rue des Beaux-Arts in Saint-Germain-des-Prés. This was such a wonderful introduction to Paris: the hotel that Oscar Wilde stayed in till his death and one that had become as famous for the people who stayed there as it was for its incredible location right in the centre of the Left Bank.

We dropped our bags and, as our room wasn't ready, rushed back to the street, filled with excitement, to walk along the Seine and drink up the atmosphere. We hung over the walls of the wonderful river, with all its activity: the barges heading upstream and downstream, the Citadel in the distance, people walking across the most extraordinary bridges to the Right Bank. It was simply too much to take in, in one go. We turned back and walked past the hotel and into the Rue de Seine. It was mind blowing.

As we turned the corner the street opened into a vibrant and busy market with food shops and stalls—eye candy to a simple cook from Sydney: it was like walking into Charlie's Chocolate Factory except instead of wanting to eat the chocolate I just wanted to cook and taste everything I saw. There were butchers with meat that looked so amazing— incredible veal, large ribs of beef, pure white saddles of pork, the most incredible chickens. I saw my first Bresse Chicken, the famous bird of Burgundy, right there. There was rotisserie of chicken and pork rolling around, glistening with the fat as it cooked and fell to the potatoes underneath. Awesome takeaway indeed. Cheese shops full of so many beautiful cheeses of all kinds with large slabs of butter and pails of crème fraîche and cream that screamed to have a finger dipped in it. The stalls were full of plump and small vegetables and ripe sweet fruit, vibrant herbs and the most incredible asparagus I had ever seen. The green asparagus was amazing enough, but to see my first ever white asparagus was a revelation. I had seen photos before but to meet in person was almost like falling in love at that moment. There was the fishmonger too, with huge turbot, sea bass and sole and the most incredible langoustine, lobster and oysters of all kinds and shape. The charcuterie—full of terrines, cooked meats and all manner of prepared salads, bowls of celeriac remoulade. It all sent me into a total spin. Wine shops, full of wine I have lusted over my whole life and then the patisserie—oh my god, the tarts and gateaux and moulded desserts, but I couldn't stop thinking about that perfect fine apple tart, I just had to have one and as I ate it walking along the street I thought how I must sit and have a coffee, but most of all I simply thought … I must be in heaven. Oh, and with all the excitement I almost forgot my first baguette. Bread unlike any I had ever seen or tasted … crisp, white, crunchy, melting, the taste so sweet and mouth-watering. This alone would be a very good reason to come to Paris, just for a loaf of bread, but oh, what bread it is.

We returned to the hotel to find a very comfortable place to rest and then in the afternoon explored the city. What an experience. At every turn something amazing. Notre Dame—a straight-up OMG moment. The Louvre—an awesome place and the pyramid wasn't even there then. Up the Champs-Élysées to the Arc de Triomphe and over the river again to the Eiffel Tower. This is truly a city to walk around and wonder at its history and beauty. We had walked the left and right banks, had explored the Place de Madeleine, visited all the shops along Rue Saint-Honoré. We had walked for hours and rather than feeling tired, we were full of youthful excitement and focussed on dinner, but still, a couple of hours nap in the afternoon would be a good idea, right?

That first night we went to Alain Dutournier's Au Trou Gascon—not as flash as it is now but all the same a wonderful introduction to Paris. I had my first taste of real foie gras and knew it wouldn't be my last, although I can't remember much of what we ate. I know that I really enjoyed it and our first day in Paris was complete.

The next morning it was up for a walk and breakfast at a local café … freshly squeezed orange juice, one of those amazing baguettes with ham and cheese and a coffee: ah, I love Paris. The baguette arrived and we looked at each other. How could we possibly eat something so large? We clearly should have split one, but what fools were we. Within five minutes we had demolished the best sandwich I had ever had and were contemplating ordering another; only the thought of a light lunch and what we knew would be a massive Michelin-starred restaurant experience was holding us back.

We spent the day at the Louvre and again did what is best to do in Paris, walked and walked. That evening we dressed and headed out to the gardens in Paris excited to be eating at Le Pre Catelan, which was owned and run by the famous pastry chef Gaston Lenôtre. His son Patrick was the chef and, from memory, it was a two-star in those days. The food was delicious and I remember drinking a 1980 Chateaux Margot, a wine not fancied because of the wet year in Bordeaux but cheap and really delicious for a thing so young. The rest of the meal, although delicious I'm sure, hasn't stuck in my memory after all these years.

The next day we spent most of our time revisiting the markets and looking at food stores, which for me, back then, were just extraordinary as we had nothing like them in Australia. In reality, though, we were just staying calm and relaxed as the most important part of our trip so far was going to be dinner that night, our first ever three Michelin star and this was why we were here.

Our booking some months before had been made for Alain Senderens' L'Archestrate. We arrived with great excitement. Upon being seated, we simply sat and soaked up the atmosphere. Here there seemed to be service at every moment; it was clear this was different to everywhere else we had been and that it was famous for good reason. Once we started to eat, I knew we were indulging in something very special. Actually it was more than special, it was life changing. We decided on the tasting menu and the first course arrived: a little cube of fresh foie gras wrapped in cabbage and steamed; on the side was sea salt and freshly ground pepper. We were instructed to sprinkle a little of both on the cabbage then pop the foie in our mouths and eat it while still hot. Oh my god, it was amazing—the crunch of the cabbage, the hit of salt and pepper and the melt-in-the-mouth sensation and flavour of the fresh foie. This was sheer genius in such a simple way.

The next course arrived; it was a salad of lobster, duck confit and mango. The centre of the plate was warm frissee dressed in walnut oil with slices of freshly cooked lobster, cubes of pan-fried duck confit and mango surrounding the main prize. As I tasted each of these flavours on the same fork my mouth was full of a dish that could only be described as balance and harmony, simply the most delicious salad I had ever tried, but again no tricks—just great ingredients that married so well together.

Next, a sautéed piece of salmon with leek coulis. It was the first time I had tasted wild salmon and I couldn't believe what a wonderful fish it was paired with the sweet earthy leek, cooked slowly and mounted with butter. So simple, elegant and utterly delicious.

The main arrived, slices of perfectly cooked milk-fed lamb lying casually next to an assortment of beautiful little vegetables and a drizzle of some simple pan juices over the meat, almost not there at all. This was so delicious, the milky tender lamb younger than I had ever tasted, the vegetables intense—turnip, carrot and radish that tasted as if they had just come from the ground, each mouthful bursting with flavour.

I can't seem to remember dessert on that night, perhaps the wine had kicked in, perhaps by then I was overwhelmed and by that course my life had changed.

We went on to eat some amazing food in some great three-star restaurants all over France, but this was the one that changed my cooking forever.

I had been cooking away, making French Provençale food at Barrenjoey House in Palm Beach at that stage of my life. My father had armed me with the knowledge that great produce was everything in cooking; I had a great love of Chinese food and from that moment on I realised I could release my own produce-driven style of cooking and it could be serious and could be world class too. In that one meal I understood that great produce didn't need secondary sauces, albeit good ones, it needed to be expressed by its own true flavour and it needed to be light and intense at the same time. Meat and seafood needed a relationship with vegetables and herbs and a simple drop of juice from the pan was more important than any stock-based sauce.

From the day I arrived back in the kitchen in Palm Beach on a cold June day, I started cooking Neil Perry's food, something I hadn't done until that wonderful and life changing trip to France.

FRANCES MAYES had written six books of poetry and *The Discovery of Poetry* before she bought a house in Italy and spontaneously began writing prose. *Under the Tuscan Sun, Bella Tuscany, Every Day in Tuscany*, two photo texts, the novels *Swan* and *A Year in the World* followed. Her books have been translated into over forty languages. Recently she gathered together the recipes from many feasts and published *The Tuscan Sun Cookbook*. She and her poet husband, Edward Mayes, live in North Carolina in a community of writers and artists, and in Cortona, Tuscany. *Under Magnolia: A Southern Memoir* will be published in 2014

DEVIL IN A BLUE APRON

Frances Mayes

A long, long time ago, before glorious farmers' markets bloomed, before the non-stop Food Network, recipe blogs, celebrity cooks trying not to look foolish on *Iron Chef,* before the proliferation of excellent food magazines, and even before rampant obesity (resulting from torturous attitudes toward eating), before foams, gluten crazes, before food became cult, and way before every third *mas,* villa, and farm kitchen in France and Italy became a cooking school, I journeyed far to study with Simone Beck in Provence.

What propelled me across the Atlantic in those dim years? My husband was sailing all the time he was not working. My daughter was entranced with her horse. I often felt that I was flying around my room, a bird come in through the chimney. I wanted to be a writer but kept cooking instead. *Go somewhere new,* I thought. My friend Jeannette called to tell me about the cooking classes and before she finished the sentence, I said, 'Let's go.'

We were five at Simone Beck's honey-colored house, La Campanette, in the hills above Grasse: Jeannette, also from San Francisco, two pretty and accomplished young women from Atlanta, and a woman from South Africa who was sent there while her boyfriend went on vacation with his wife. Jeannette and I had cooked our way through *Mastering the Art of French Cooking*, which Simca co-authored with Julia Child. We were adept at dinner parties featuring cream soups, veal Prince Orloff, Grand Marnier soufflé, and other time-consuming, flamboyant, delicious recipes. We loved *Simca's Cuisine*, her straightforward approach, and immediately liked her no-nonsense rigor in the kitchen. On the first day she gave each of us an apron that matched her impression of us. Mine was plain blue, while the others got charming flowers and stripes. Simca was cordial to us, but not friendly. When Cathy from Atlanta asked one question too many, Simca cut her off with 'Are we going to measure or are we going to cook?' We worked in the morning, and then enjoyed a sumptuous lunch on the terrace. Fish mousseline with hollandaise, pizza with pastry crust, sole in ring mold with *velouté*, and various sausages in brioche—not exactly Sunday night suppers but still easy and fun. Simca demonstrated. We were assigned small tasks. We took notes. We did not clean up.

If one of us asked a question she usually looked incredulous through her tinted glasses and curtly said, 'But you have it in de *Mastering*,' as if we should have memorized the whole tome. But I was learning how to beat egg whites in a copper bowl until I could hold the bowl upside down over my head—that's how you know they're stiff enough. I learned to boil chicken stock uncovered so that it reduces and concentrates. We made airy rolled soufflé filled with crab. Never brown shallots, just melt them. She preferred metal spoons because wooden ones 'always have some fat on them'. I learned to keep my knives sharp and dry. Never waste anything. I saw her save the whites when only yolks were needed. Leftover bread became crumbs. Shells of shrimp went into the broth. In that plain kitchen, I acquired life-changing habits. Many small changes add up to revolutionary change. She respected ingredients as a writer respects words. Frugal as she was, the table was set with largesse. Her *trucs* and scoldings and care gently seeped into my hands and made me more aware as I stood at the stove. I began to see the process of cooking as an art and a practice, not a means to an end. I began to love the battered pans, wooden bowls, a particular slotted spoon, colanders and baskets. My tools.

French desserts descended to earth from a certain corner of heaven. We constructed then devoured Simca's toffee-based tart of packed-down apples (*tartin des pommes)*, chocolate gateau garnished with cherries in kirsch, and a dense chocolaty-chocolate mousse without cream. She taught the French way with meringue—cook it over hot water then, through a pastry tube, pipe decorative rings around fruit or lemon tarts. (Way too much trouble.)

I could not know then that from Simca's dessert repertoire, one recipe would come to stand for all the tastes, aromas and bliss of my time at La Campanette—Le Diabolo, a flat, dense, unassuming chocolate cake. Simca took the recipe from her mother's little black notebook. I recall vividly the first taste: the inner essence of chocolate, sweet, with a touch of almond, and buttery with a slight hit of bitterness from the coffee in the frosting. *A complex cake*, I thought. *I don't know if I've ever made a complex cake before*. The ones I knew were straightforward, except for my mother's formidable Lane Cake, which I'd never attempted.

The name, too, is complex. I assumed *diabolo* meant 'devil'. But a French devil is *diable*. Italian and Spanish devils are *diavolo* and *diablo*. Going way back to the Greek, a *diabolos* was a liar. For later Christian writers, the word meant 'the liar who speaks against God', therefore, a devil. I can see why one might think of that deep chocolate as diabolical, as in *the devil made me do it*. But why Simca's mother spelled her cake *diabolo* remains a mystery, and we can't ask now. Perhaps it's dialect or an obsolete spelling. Maybe she liked juggling, because now the word 'diabolo' refers to a nifty device for a juggler's tricks, a sort of double cup joined at the bottom and strung between two sticks. When we separated eggs, Simca had us break the egg into our hands, letting the whites slip through our fingers while the yolks remained whole in our palms. 'You must be very sure of your eggs,' she cautioned. Cooking can be a bit like juggling.

Made in a round baking pan, the ancient devil stands two-inches high, at most. Although in her cookbook Simca lists an American chocolate, you can be sure that in her French kitchen she used chocolate from a special shop in Paris. Little flour is called for, and ground almonds keep the batter from ambitious rising. The top becomes slightly crusty and the middle stays moist—more than moist, but not quite creamy. 'You must be careful not to overbake,' she warned. One minute past noon is midnight, some writer said, and that's true here. The soft and delectable texture can turn dry and brittle in a flash.

As soon as it cools, you pour over it a simple coffee-based chocolate butter cream, thin but intense. Guests put down their forks and look at you as though you've unveiled The Winged Victory. A sliver will do—this is not the same thing at all as the much-loved towering layer 1-2-3-4 cakes of my youth. They were slathered in luscious thick icing. Discovering Le Diabolo was sort of like the moment of recognition when you're dressed in blue flounces and someone wearing black Prada walks in. You get it. When something is this good, you don't need much. Sometimes I ring the cake with raspberries, but, really, what's the point? Le Diabolo needs no embellishment. In my kitchens, I have turned out Le Diabolo onto the same white Wedgwood plate for my daughter's birthdays, endless dinner parties, potlucks, even funerals. Now my daughter bakes it for her family, and I've passed on the recipe to many friends, who, in turn, have handed it to others. On that first day, however, my history with Le Diabolo was unwritten. I ate each bite slowly, slowly, savoring every tender morsel.

In the afternoons, we meandered to Biot, Fayence, Vence. We were allowed in the kitchens of the Michelin-starred chefs in the area. Sharp-eyed Simca took us to markets and taught us to buy the right fish—look at its eyes and the shimmer of the scales—and cunning little cheeses wrapped in grape leaves, and olives, and small purple artichokes. We learned to drink *kir royale* (and I'd thought Champagne was glamorous) on the terrace at evening, where, with Simca and her husband Jean, we were sometimes joined by Julia herself and her courtly husband Paul. The effervescent sunset light in the Kir seemed to have absorbed the color of the rays raking across the distant hills. Julia was interested in how we 'girls' were getting on. Her high voice thrilled us, and although we were shy around her, we had fun trying to imitate her when we were back in our quarters.

I was seduced by the gentle landscape and by the idea of a life in the countryside. The air was balmy. As we drove, I was dazzled by the golden, perched villages, the Matisse chapel, and the acres of roses cultivated by perfume makers. We sometimes stopped, as evening fell, at a small square and dined outdoors under greening plane trees. Biting into *poulet à l'estragon,* I devoured, too, the way of life behind it. I thought, *I'd like to live this way.*

The trip was brief. Poppies spread like a brushfire all over the fields. Never had I seen such a marvel. How is it that some people get to *live* their everyday lives here? I fancied as I packed my bag that I could fold into my clothes the scent of the nearby roses. Simca's book was dog-eared and spattered. Provençal fabric sacks of herbs did penetrate all my summery dresses. En route back to the US, on a stop in Paris, I madly purchased a copper pot, chocolate (grocery store chocolate was *over*), individual cylindrical molds for *soufflés d'Alençon,* vanilla powder, various extracts, a nutmeg grinder, and all sizes of tart pans, some of which, eons later, still have the stickers on them. Who knew when I'd ever pass that way again?

I went home. I enrolled in graduate school. I became a writer. Years after, I bought a honey-and-rose-colored house on a hillside in Tuscany, where I love to cook and entertain my friends. I grow roses. The view to the south falls away into olive and grape terraces, and a small tower anchors the distant hills. I must have baked Simca's chocolate cake five hundred times.

DAVID MAS MASUMOTO is an organic farmer, newspaper columnist, and the author of six books, including *Epitaph for a Peach*, *Wisdom of the Last Farmer*, and the cookbook *The Perfect Peach: Recipes and Stories from the Masumoto Family Farm*. He grows certified organic peaches, nectarines, and raisins near Fresno, California.

THE BOYS OF SUMMER

David Mas Masumoto

Other than the occasional whiffs of aromas, little came over the wall. A large, 10-foot-high barrier separated our house from another world. I knew people were cooking on the other side; I could smell oil and fried food. Like a siren, a simmering scent infused with an earthy aroma drifted in the air. A pungent fragrance of sweat and smoke piqued my curiosity.

So when the soccer ball sailed over to our side, I was given an invitation to explore. Soccer balls flew everywhere in Brazil during that June in 1971. The year before, at the World Cup in Mexico, Brazil had assembled one of the greatest teams ever. Led by Pele, they won their third World Cup in commanding style. Brazil soared and remained soccer crazy.

That summer, I landed in Brazil as a naive sixteen-year-old high-school exchange student for a summer abroad. I had left our family farm near the small town of Del Rey, in the middle of California, nestled in the rich agricultural San Joaquin Valley.

I journeyed to Salvador, Brazil, and quickly felt lost. I knew a little Spanish, mainly a few bad words my school buddies in California had taught me, but I comprehended even less Portuguese. As a farm boy, I understood our peaches, nectarines and raisins but my knowledge helped little with passion fruit, mangos or coconuts. These Brazilian crops were foreign with amazingly fresh, yet alien, flavors.

However, I could play soccer and sweat with the best of them. As I retrieved the soccer ball, heads quickly popped over the top of the wall and peered down at me. The brown and black faces were signaling; they yelled and pointed, wanting me to toss the ball back. Instead, I unleashed a solid kick and the ball soared back over. The kids laughed with surprise. They immediately launched the ball back over the fence and howled even louder as we played a new game with the fence barrier as our net.

My Brazilian home was built on a gentle hill. Terraced levels of housing were neatly divided by streets that meandered on our side of the fence. My host family was considered upper class and wealthy. Brazil in the 1970s had no middle class. You were either rich or poor. Two servants helped in our kitchen and with housework.

A few kids started taunting me to kick harder. They called me '*Japa*'. They thought I was a Japanese Brazilian, probably from São Paulo, one of the largest and richest cities in Brazil. Like the Japanese who initially immigrated to America, Brazilian Japanese came as farm laborers to work on coffee plantations. They struggled, were classified as non-white, deemed unable to assimilate, and clung to their own ways.

My summer (their winter) was to be spent in Salvador, a large city in the state of Bahia, located in northeastern Brazil. This was once the colonial capital and the port of entry for African slaves. The climate was tropical, hot and humid, and Salvador carried the reputation of being slow and easygoing, with a negative connotation of being lazy. I understood some of this— it reminded me of my California hometown of Del Rey, a sleepy little town surrounded by farms, stigmatized with a culture of slowness, as if we were all dull farmers and stupid farm workers. And Bahia was also considered home to crazy characters.

One of the kids launched a monster soccer kick to my side. Sudden gusts of wind changed the trajectory of our game. The soccer ball sailed over my house and down the street—along with a fresh aroma of something cooking beyond the wall. I scampered down the road to retrieve the ball and discovered a place where the wall had crumbled, a gateway into another world. I followed the scent with soccer ball in hand.

A mud and dirt road served as a makeshift soccer field and part of the dividing line along with the fence. I discovered what had been hidden from me: the favela, the slums of Brazil.

Houses were piled on top of each other, stacked in random fashion. Older homes with deteriorating walls and a mildew gray color stood at the base of the sloping terrain. The homes seemed to grow like weeds along the steep hillside—a dense growth of vivid reds, off whites with occasional yellow and blue hues. Many structures appeared to be made of bricks with mortar sloppily oozing out the edges. The collection looked like a house of cards, tenuously stacked as high as possible before tumbling down.

The few streets were half dirt and rock, some asphalt. They wound up the grade, getting lost in the mass of homes. The favela looked like a river of the poor, following a gully down from the mountainside, trapped between ridges and embankments too steep for stable buildings, snaking down the natural terrain, then tumbling onto the lower plain but abruptly stopping, often at a wide road or barrier. I lived on the other side of those divides.

In the favela, people roamed the streets and walkways. They stood in wide windows that had no glass. They traveled with bicycles and in groups. Some hung laundry to dry, others carried cans of water and wooden crates. They moved in a slow dance, a daily progression of life, ants toiling to get by and survive.

Even though it was winter in June, the humidity combined with warmth (about 27°C or 80°F), creating a climate of skin. In the wealthy parts of Salvador, most people wore shorts and short sleeves; here in the favela, males were shirtless, women in tank tops. Shoes were optional for most; others wore light slippers or sandals. I must have looked like a true foreigner with a light shirt, jeans, tennis shoes and socks.

The air was filled with the aroma of people—a mix of sweat and sewage, of mud and the morning rains. But I could also smell food. Out of an open window, smoke wandered out and filled the street with the scent of spices, grilled meat and vegetables. I could breathe in shrimp and garlic, rice and beans. Walk past another door and my eyes were greeted by ripe mango and papaya. Although it was afternoon, morning coffee lingered in one doorway along with the stale scent of last night's beer. I had imagined that the poor in foreign countries used open fires, but here most had small gas burners or electric hot plates. (Later

I learned that in Brazilian slums free electrical hookups were tolerated.)

Bahian food was being prepared. Many homes were frying *acarajé*. I had eaten this deep-fried bread-like staple made from black-eyed peas at my host family's table. Their black servants knew this dish well and were happy that I liked their food, especially when served with shrimp or tomatoes. I had seen street vendors, black women in crisp white dresses and headscarves, set up sidewalk stands where they molded the food and fried them for sale. My family insinuated that *acarajé* was poor people's food but they wanted me to taste Bahia. Now that I was walking in the favela, I was consuming it all.

I peeked into one kitchen and saw a black kettle simmering with a stew of beans, big beans and some rice, all colored a very bright orange-red. I would learn that the color came from a palm oil called *dende*. It had arrived along with the African slaves hundreds of years earlier, transplanting a food culture to this place. I couldn't quite understand why with such a hot and humid climate, they served heavy stews and deep-fried foods. But many things in the favela were confusing and yet made sense. This was the place of the poor, just a few feet away from my house and yet a world apart.

Was it any different than my California farm home, where undocumented alien Mexicans worked the fields, hiding from authorities, part of the invisible army of hands behind our peaches and nectarines? Our workers, for their *lonche* morning break, brought out little gas burners to heat stew and warm tortillas. Even in our blazing 100-degree summer harvest days, a stew with beans and rice fueled these laborers.

Like their Brazilian counterparts, my Japanese grandparents had immigrated to toil in the fields, a wave of silent workers, allowed into a country to fill a labor void. Perhaps I had more in common with the poor of both America and this favela than I had ever imagined.

At some point the worn soccer ball was returned to the Brazilian kids from the other side of the wall. Most were younger than me, shirtless, barefoot, dark and tanned, curly black hair with huge grins. They now called me '*Americano*' and understood I was different. A few crowded around, asking me something I could not translate. Others didn't care, they had their ball back.

Nearby, I first heard the tinkle of small bells. They were attached to an old, dingy cart with large bicycle-like front wheels that supported a metal ice box, once painted green and yellow.

'*Picoléeeee, Pi-co-léee!*' shouted the vendor, a man in his thirties with dark, weathered skin. Then he whistled, a high-pitched breathy signal that the popsicle man had arrived.

Picolé was a frozen treat on a stick, either fruit- or dairy-based. Strawberry, passion fruit, mango or coconut-flavored juices were used, sometimes with pieces of fruit suspended in the ice pop. Vanilla and chocolate were the typical flavors of ice-cream-like bars. The refreshing delight was held by the flat stick protruding from one end. The wooden handle was wider than the American popsicle stick and fit the hands of the young, the old, and even foreigners.

In Brazil, I experienced my first street food. Back in California, no vendor walked the rural roads by our farm. No carts or ice-cream trucks stopped for a break on a steamy day. Until my arrival in Salvador, I had zero experience of the anticipation when you first heard the tinkling bell or familiar cry of a vendor who brought relief from daily life.

The *picolé* man had stopped. He looked tired, weary from a day of walking the streets, hawking his goods. Water was dripping from the rusting corners of the aging metal box; inside the block of ice was melting.

A small group of boys crowded around the *picolé* man. They spoke in a rapid exchange. The vendor then reached deep into his box as the boys congregated, arms reaching inward. One boy pointed at me, the man looked up and grinned at the foreigner.

Then a boy, about ten, with a heaping headful of hair, brought a *picolé* to me. He quickly stripped off the wax-paper wrapping, letting it fall to the ground, then extended his arm in my direction, offering me the treat.

As I reached for it, I wondered: who was my new friend? Did he pay for the ice pop, my reward for returning the soccer ball? Only a few other kids had a *picolé*; most watched with open mouths.

I guessed the yellow bar might be mango flavor, something I had never tasted in California. The juices were already dripping down the sides. The surface glistened in the bright sun. Smiles surrounded me.

Then I noticed the ants. They were suspended in the frozen liquid along one side. There, the ice bar was slightly flatter, with a smooth surface. About ten creatures were captured in that space, their final movements locked in ice.

Once I saw photos in a magazine of the big-ass ants of Brazil. The article explained that they were protein, a delicacy, and huge, up to an inch in length. During the rainy season, when the ants swarmed, people ran around waving sheets, knocking them out of the air, grabbing the bodies and ripping off heads, plunking the remaining body parts into a jar. Later, they'd fry them in butter or oven-roast the morsels. I was fixated by the story.

My *picolé* ants were not that big. They looked like normal ants except they were in a popsicle.

I looked up and a bunch of the kids were watching me. I froze, not sure what to do. Did I insult these boys and toss the half-melted-bottom-of-the-cart leftover? Or did someone buy this for me, an act of kindness poor people often display— those with the least sometimes give the most.

I thought of my elementary school in Del Rey. Poor kids often brought odd foods from home. Once I took some leftover sushi with nori from home and my Mexican school buddies went wild—some hated it, others made fun of me, a few thought it was cool. I thought the same of their menudo, fried pork rinds, and *chapulines*, or grasshoppers.

So I ate my *picolé*. The kids went back to their soccer. I watched for a few minutes—they were way too fast, too talented, too experienced for me. I then quietly slipped back through the wall to my side.

A few weeks later I departed Brazil. But before I left, I took the bus by myself (my host family worried, fearing I'd get lost) to downtown Salvador and spent the day walking, buying street food, and watching the people of Bahia on the beach and in a park. I thought about the favela and the poor in America, especially in our farming valley of California. It took traveling to a foreign country to discover home.

I bought more *picolé*, without ants. I sat in a park and witnessed two men fighting and dancing—my initial exposure to capoeira, which I later learned was a martial art form blending dance, music and the history of African slaves and their struggle for identity. The two men were sweating, sometimes accidentally striking each other; occasionally they paused, drank cachaça (Brazilian rum), then fought more. Crazy. Like people warned me about Bahia.

That summer, I returned to our family farm and our struggle with the politics of the unionization of farm workers. The United Farm Workers were fighting for rights, the air was toxic with anger and protest. Our small farm was visited by pickets and organizers. I was confused and young: since when was eating a political act? It was and still is.

My dad was crushed; our family were once farm workers—my father tried to be fair and understood the hard, physical work firsthand. He couldn't understand why the public was demonizing farmers. He felt we were all poor.

That summer I changed in a slight but significant way. The meals in Bahia, the aromas of the favela, and the *picolé* with ants all helped me realize food had meaning. We were farmers and our peaches were more than just peaches. Food embodied story, which included the poor. Culture was wrapped in a meal or snack. No longer was food simply food.

KAUI HART HEMMINGS' first novel, *The Descendants*, was published in 22 countries and made into an Oscar-winning film. Her next novel, *The Possibilities*, will be out in 2014. Follow her travels at http://instagram.com/kauihart/ and https://www.facebook.com/KauiHartHemmings.

A COFFEE CEREMONY

Kaui Hart Hemmings

I drank coffee every morning, usually at the kitchen table while checking my email. I'd drink it while walking around the house, herding the family toward their various checkpoints—breakfast, teeth, backpack, lunch—before work and school in Honolulu, Hawaii. Then I'd sit down again with my coffee. Laptop open. Morning news on. I almost always drank alone.

My solo java routine was interrupted when we went to Addis Ababa to finalize the adoption of our son. We had already travelled there less than a month ago, but this time we'd be able to bring him home.

There's a lot to do in Addis, a city perched on a plateau, bustling with students, markets, buses and goats. We visited Haile Selassie's former palace, the museum that housed the infamous Lucy. We trekked down Bole Road, explored the nightlife, but it's hard to be a tourist when you're staying in a guesthouse with adoptive parents and children, some of whom have no one coming for them. Our sightseeing had more to do with wanting to know a place, store it somehow for future hunger.

There was a lot of down time, time in which we couldn't go too far, time filled with coffee.

It's ritual here, a way to gather, and it's frequently drawn out for long periods of time. In coffee shops it seems people would sit and drink and talk for hours, never hunched over a laptop, rarely alone.

Coffee is woven into the society, into the history of Ethiopia, its origin. I learn that the growing and picking process of the beans involves over 12 million Ethiopians and produces over two-thirds of the country's earnings, and I have to say that when I get back to the US I am bereft. I'm not a coffee snob, but the richness of it, the depth, is unfindable, or I just haven't taken the time.

Time. That's what this is really about. Taking the time to realize what you're doing, what you're drinking.

>>>—

'It's like their happy hour,' I said to my husband, who rarely drinks coffee at home, but did so regularly here.

'At all hours,' he said.

We watched people laugh and talk, similar to the way you do with friends in bars, discussing your day, your problems, the large and mundane stuff of life, chatter fueled by the buzz.

Every day, at least twice a day, we went to the Daily Cup, walking through the dusty streets. We'd go with another couple who had adopted a child from Rwanda, and we'd sit and talk and drink, trying to know a place, through its food and rituals and local clientele. We were cafe flies. We were outsiders, bewildered, far from home, trying our best to mingle.

On our last day before the thirty-two-hour flight home, we were introduced to the coffee ceremony, when I realized that coffee could get even slower.

It's a common practice, not necessarily done on special occasions, but at our guesthouse, the staff were doing the ceremony as a way to say goodbye.

My seven-year-old daughter and I sat in the living room, watching the women who work at the guesthouse roasting the beans over a small charcoal stove. The smoke mixed with the burning incense, making it seem like something sumptuous and earthy was on fire. The two women were attentive to it, jostling and stirring, whisking away.

'We get the oil out,' she said. 'And then we—' She made a motion with her wrist that I took for grinding by hand, then stirred and shook the husks away. When the coffee beans turned black she ground them by pestle and a long-handled mortar.

My daughter was bored—she was here for the popcorn that is always served with the coffee. I told her boredom was good for her. We watched the grinding and then the stirring into the clay coffee pot.

'Jebena,' the younger woman said, tapping the pot, which was round at the bottom with a straw lid.

Other guests came into the living room area. Music was playing and we talked about the days we had, and what was in store for us when we got home. Our son, up from his nap, was brought in by the nurse. He was so at ease in my arms. I smelled the top of his head, locking eyes with my husband, and I think you'd assume this was a tender moment, but our look also communicated bewilderment and awe. This was our ten-month-old son who we were about to bring home, whose last eight months of life had been in one tiny room, and sometimes a small outdoor courtyard where he was entranced by a single tree growing on the other side of the barbed wall.

We were completely out of our world, about to take him out of his, and during my time here I kept wondering how to bring a part of this city home—for us, for our son, for our family.

The coffee ceremony was satisfying some of this yearning. The women were singing, the smoke was in the air, and then the coffee was being served expertly—the pot held high above the cup, and I felt like I was part of an archaic ceremony, an induction of sorts, and the ritual seemed to be just what I needed to mark this time, to reduce many emotions into a taste, into an unforgettable blend.

I took a sip of the coffee—it was beautiful, though probably more so because of the process itself, the gift of it and the time it took, the elegant steps. It was a kind of culinary tai chi, though not quiet or solemn—I wouldn't have liked it as much. The women spoke loudly—and they were usually quiet in the kitchen and soft-spoken with us. People were laughing, kids playing on the floor.

The coffee was making another round and the translator told us that after this, one more cup would be served, the grounds are brewed three times.

'*Awel* is first cup,' he said. 'Then *kale'i*. The third is *bereka*.'

I didn't think I could take another. Just one cup felt like three shots of espresso.

'It is rude to stop halfway,' the translator said, as if reading my (and perhaps everyone's) mind. 'The third serving is a blessing.'

Well, then. I kept drinking, wanting to be both polite and blessed, and wishing the same could be said for a third glass of wine. Voices were getting louder, laughter seemed more deep and true. We sat for more than an hour, and it made me think of all the times I carefully prepared dinner only to have it virtually chugged, the set table abandoned within twenty minutes. I wanted to take this ritual home with us. I wanted to take back the slowness.

I was on the last cup. There was a lift in my voice, my face and heart. I got the sensation of being so far from home, and yet finally embraced—which always seems to happen when you're about to leave a place. We were embarking on something, changing the voltage of our lives.

Food and drink is so much more than food and drink. When we consume them we are engaging in a backstory—the effort and attention, the craft and history, the community and connection, and the ritual itself, which harks back to unknown people and places. A coffee ceremony—I see us from a distance, a nook on the planet, and like the aroma and smoke: rising, blending, disappearing all together.

Our son is three now. I drink my coffee with him in the morning. I still bustle around, making lunches, checking email, and he sits at his little table eating his cereal and he tells me in his somewhat Italian-sounding voice: 'Sit, Mommy sit. Right here. Sit,' and I sit and I slow down, and I drink the things behind the coffee, remembering that moment. Food, a feast, a single bite, a sip—they can uncork those memories wherever you are. You can take it with you.

NAOMI DUGUID is the author of many award-winning books about food and travel. Her most recent, *Burma: Rivers of Flavor*, celebrates the food cultures of Burma in recipes, stories, and photos. To learn more, visit her website naomiduguid.com.

MEAT ON THE HOOF

Naomi Duguid

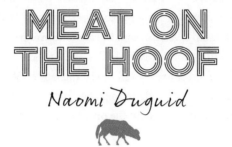

When I was a kid, every two years we'd travel out west to visit my grandparents, always in the summertime, and always by train. They lived in far northern British Columbia, where they'd settled after the First World War, homesteading on a quarter section of land, living in a log cabin full of books. They had no telephone, no running water, no electricity. Their water came from the creek; their garden vegetables (hardy crops were all that grew that far north) were stored in the root cellar; their fruit (gooseberries and raspberries and crabapples, as well as wild-gathered berries) was made into jams or preserves by my grandmother, all on her woodstove. Every year my granddad would shoot one moose, which my grandmother 'canned' in glass jars and which helped feed the family through the winter.

Right behind the house, on the other side of the fence that marked the edge of the garden, lay miles of government range. It was thick, almost impenetrable forest, 'the bush' as we called it. The only way through the bush was on trails that had been laboriously cut by my granddad. When he was younger he used them to get to his traplines in the winter. Well into his eighties he still used them to go cut firewood every year for the woodstoves that were the only form of heating in the house.

One August morning long ago my brother and I rode out into that bush with my mother and her brother Greg, looking for moose. My brother was 15; I'd just turned 13. I was bareback on Timber, a tall bright bay gelding who was a comfortable ride, with nicely padded withers. The others had saddles, western saddles: my brother on my granddad's horse, Sam, my mother on a young, barely broken mare called Sunset, and my uncle Greg on Sunset's mother, Susie, a wall-eyed skittish pinto.

We were headed to the high country around the Dome, a rocky hill four or five miles east. It was a wide-open area where Greg and my mother thought we'd find moose, or at least traces of them.

Greg had made a trail up to the Dome about ten years earlier. It hadn't been used for a while and was very overgrown. The going was slow but beautiful in a dense-bush green and fertile kind of way. Branches and leaves would whip us in the face if we didn't pay attention; 'duck!' was an ongoing call from the person in front to the person behind. The real obstacles were the windfalls, big trees that had fallen over and now blocked the trail. Each time we came to a windfall we'd have to find our way around, through dense bushes and other trees, a tedious process, scratchy sometimes, and awkward.

The bush always felt claustrophobic to me, a place to escape from. And so I was very relieved when we finally came up out of the thick, clogged greenness and into the open, green meadows near the hump of the Dome. Suddenly there was light, and a view.

The details of the first part of the day are now just simple snapshots in my memory: the musky familiar smell of sweaty horse as we loosened the girths when we stopped for lunch; making a fire to heat water in the kettle we'd brought, and then the luxury of sandwiches and tea as the horses meandered around, foraging for mouthfuls of grass; scrambling up the rock of the Dome and looking all around at 360 degrees of wild landscape, as Greg parsed it with binoculars, searching for likely moose haunts. We could see for miles. The mountains of the coastal range and the huge beautiful glaciered bulk of Hudson's Bay Mountain framed the view to the west, and greenness undulated away from us in all directions.

We rode around the high open muskeg country in the afternoon, seeing traces of moose, but nothing recent. Then as the shadows lengthened we reluctantly started back along the trail, the light dimming immediately under the dense tree canopy. I was daydreaming along when suddenly there was a bang, and I heard the sound of crashing and more crashing off to the left ahead. Greg had spotted a moose in the bad light, grabbed his rifle, and shot it. In all his time hunting one or two moose per year to feed his family he never used more than one bullet per animal. This time was no exception. But his shot had hit the lung, we discovered later, so the animal made it a good fifty or sixty feet off the trail before collapsing. I couldn't imagine how he'd seen her, let alone got off an accurate shot.

Then there we were in the rapidly failing light with a moose to locate and to butcher. We tied the horses to trees and headed into the bush, up and over one fallen tree, a walk along another, looking for the clearest route to where we thought the moose had ended up. Finally there she was. She was still hot, of course, tumbled awkwardly over a small log, her legs tangled, and quite dead. There was a silence, an absence; the life no longer breathed in her. Now she was a carcass. And she was a logistical and practical problem, a treasure of food to not waste.

It's a big responsibility, butchering. First chore: gut the animal. Yards of intestines, green with half-digested leaves and grass and steaming-warm in the cool air, came spilling out of the first incision. It took a while to sort through the belly, in the course of which the intestines got nicked and the stench of fermenting greens enveloped us. No fun. Once the intestines and stomach were moved aside, Greg could get at the organs he wanted to retrieve. We had several burlap bags, large ones, and into one went the kidneys and dark red-brown bulk of the liver. The heart, so big, went into the other, later joined by the long dense weight of the tongue.

The only way to manage that size of carcass is to cut off the unwanted pieces (legs below the knees, and also the head), and divide the body into quarters. Working with his hatchet and his knife, Greg got the carcass halved, then separated off each of the quarters. He worked fast and deftly, but still it took a long time. With the shinbone section of the legs gone, each quarter was a huge floppy weight of meat (150 pounds or more) attached to a length of leg bone.

And so off we set, my brother and I, to haul the first forequarter out to the trail. We each had two hands on the leg, gripping tightly. We hauled it across the ground a short way then reached the first of three or four fallen trees that lay between us and the trail. We did several 'one-two-three-HEAVEs!' before we managed to get the quarter up onto the tree. It balanced there for a moment like a heavy rug, before it fell forward and down with a kind of sickening slither-flop. And so it went, the hauling, the 1-2-3 heave, the moment of rest at the top, and the slide onward.

I remember grinning with relief and satisfaction at my brother when we finally made it out with our first quarter, and his grin back. But then came a feeling of dread as I thought of the weight of work that still faced us: three more quarters to haul. In the end we did two more and my mother and Greg did the last one. The burlap bags of organ meat came too, of course. We left the rest for the scavengers in the bush.

Greg decided that we'd leave two of the quarters there, as well as the bag with the liver and the kidneys. That meant throwing a rope up over a tree branch, then slowly hoisting the quarters up until they hung high above us, hopefully safe from hungry wolverines or other animals. The plan was that we'd come back for them the next day.

And the other two quarters? They couldn't go on Susie, who wouldn't let any meat near her, nor on my brother's horse, Sam, who was also skittish about it. I was bareback so I could carry only the sack of heart and tongue. That left Sunset, the slightly goofy young mare my mother was riding, to carry two quarters, about 350 pounds of meat. She stood quivering as we lashed them onto the saddle horn. They hung down in front of the saddle, one on each side, and rubbed her at every step.

I remember watching her eyes roll as my mother got on, adding yet more weight to her. Would she buck and protest? It seemed likely. But perhaps because the day had already tired her out, she stayed docile under her load as we headed down the trail. It was late night by then, the darkness opaque under the forest canopy. Greg led the way. From my place at the back I caught very occasional glimpses of the white patches on Susie's pinto rump. Mostly, though, there was just darkness and a few sounds: the muffled thud of the horses' hooves on the dirt, the breathing of my horse Timber, the hoot of an owl.

I fell into a dazed kind of trance, one hand clutching the burlap sack with its load of meat, the other loosely holding the reins, and my head nodding with each stride. Life and being were reduced to the now, the physical sensations of the horse moving under me, the feel of his hide, the weight of the sack, the coarse familiar texture of his mane, and the supple leather of the reins. And beyond that there was nothing but the horses ahead of me in the dark, and the scent of the bush at night, a chilly moist woods smell.

It took an eternity, that ride. And then sometime after midnight, like a hallucination, a flicker of light appeared on the trail ahead of Greg. It was my granddad, who had come walking up the trail on foot carrying a lantern, worried that something had happened to us. He refused a ride back, and so we went on ahead of him the last half mile, to unload Sunset's meat and to rub the horses down and put them out to pasture.

I have no other memory of our arrival except of the relief I felt as I crawled into my bed in the warm silence of my grandparents' log house.

The rest of the work—or perhaps I should say the rest of our obligation to the moose—came next day. Greg and my mother went back up the trail early in the morning to get the other quarters and the rest of the organ meat, which had survived untouched up in the tree. My aunt spent the day cutting the meat up, and various kids and I helped wrap each piece in butcher paper and label it. The meat would go into their meat locker, a large storage freezer in town, food for the family that fall and winter. My aunt made a slow-simmered pot roast that night—the moose meat cooked through and succulent—accompanied by her pillowy homemade bread and followed by fruit pies. We were ten or 11 people around the table, digging in with pleasure, grateful for all of it.

The moose story returns to me from time to time now, all these years later. What's this about? I wonder. In part, as with all momentous events lived, it's time-travel that pulls me there. Both my mother and my brother are long dead, and in reliving this story I get to be with them again, working shoulder to shoulder, feeling their energy.

But the deeper pull of the story, I've come to realize, is that it's about life and death and human responsibility. Once the moose was killed it was up to us to take care of the meat, to not waste it. The death had to be earned, perhaps that's one way of saying it. My uncle and mother were in charge, and my brother and I did as we were told, just as children have for generations helped with the harvest of meat, fish, grain or produce. And in the moment there is no questioning, no room for doubt or tiredness or holding back. There is only necessity.

Author and documentary filmmaker **TAMASIN DAY-LEWIS** has published 12 books and writes on all subjects related and unrelated to food. Her forthcoming book, *Smart Tart*, is a crowd-funded book and can be found at www.unbound.co.uk

THE CATCH
Tamasin Day-Lewis

When you are young there are continents of new flavours to
explore. The caches of sophistication, of knowing golden
Oscietra from black beady Beluga, foie gras d'oie from canard,
the Widow Cliquot from Cristal—these are things you either
get to know about or they never cross your culinary threshold.
Food snobbery and good taste are not necessarily bedfellows:
aspirations and connoisseurship can be a million miles apart.

I didn't know, when I was allowed to stay up to the dinner
table one night, that picking my grandfather's grouse bones
was not a common experience for a nine-year-old, but what I
did know, innately, having been inculcated unbeknownst to
me with the virtues of a good table from an early age, was that
my tastebuds had come as pretty close to heaven as they ever
had and that grouse was not a realm of taste I had previously
entered into.

It was like shrapnel, a bombshell exploding in my mouth.

It was surprising, rich, rare, gamey, bloody, only back then I had neither the adjectives nor the knowledge to describe it.

It wasn't yet a memory. It was an experience.

It led me to believe there must be other similar experiences that would hit me explosively and knock me off my culinary everyday feet. And in due course there were.

To begin with, you string together the rare jewels of edible experience like you are mapping the unmapped for the very first time, a frontiersman, a budding gourmand, adding and subtracting, snipe with woodcock, scented mirabelles with Alfonso mangoes, sweetbreads, wild sea trout, salmon with their fat, coral fleshiness; sappy green or juicy white asparagus puddled in hot butter; the first artichoke, leaf after leaf, to its secret-hearted choke. The smack of salt and sea from an oyster.

Yet in Victorian London oysters were poor man's food, beef steak and oyster pie was the food of inns and trenchermen, what we now consider a luxury was an economy, like cockles, whelks, mussels, eel pie and mash. It was the Irish stew of the sea making up for in vitamins and minerals what the grinding diet of poverty and monotony eschewed, leading, as it did, to rickets, scurvy, malnutrition and death from dirty water.

Glut and gluttony, unparalleled choice, wealth and slenderness, poverty and morbid obesity, we are one planet yet several worlds of culinary extremes at the turn of this twenty-first century. From *la cucina povera*, eaten at the tables of both the rich and the poor in Puglia, to the rarefied extremes of the three-star restaurant, the food that we put into our mouths and bellies influences every area of our lives: our brains and body, our health, our pleasure and desires, our senses, our imagination, feelings, intellect and understanding, our children, our philosophy, our income. Our food defines us as people, wherever we live, whatever our attitude to it.

The excitement I have always felt about food and cooking was not, like some undimmed passion, finally extinguished once I had eaten my fill of the exotic and highly prized foods from around the world and cooked for friends, family, my three children, over four decades of cooking life.

No, the nature of excitement has merely shifted so that what once was an apogee of a dish no longer enthrals in the same way. I don't mean it disenthrals, I mean it has become part of the tapestry of my taste memory, while I have gone on searching for the perfect dish with greater attention to simplicity and truth.

Let me explain.

If I order a slice of chocolate sachertorte I order it knowing there will be less surprise but no less gratification. It was what, as a child, I most associated with pleasure: my half-term treat at Fortnum's Fountain with my indulgent grandmother and my brother, after the dentist. Accompanied by freshly squeezed orange juice and blackcurrant ice cream with a thick fan-wafer that shattered like glass on the tongue and a light cloud of cream to dip into with it, the teas we had were sacrosanct and unchanging. Whatever else was on the menu was paid no attention to.

I have been lucky enough to experience and enjoy many of the rarer and more costly foods on the planet: I have hunted for white truffles in Alba, stalked stags for a saddle or a haunch of venison, visited dairies in Provence whose rare Roves goats feed on wild thyme and are milked for little fresh cheeses rolled in *sariette*—summer savory—and the Franche-Comte for Vacherin Mont d'Or, barely contained in its hoop of cedarwood and tasting earthy, nutty, buttery, bacony in November, farm-yardy, silagey in late March.

I have eaten the bottled, preserved, dried and fresh vegetarian cuisine of Rajasthan, and saddle of hare in a garlicky *aillade* from a mad March hare that I scooped off the road in the west of Ireland and slung over my handlebars.

I have grown quince, fig, damson, mulberry and crabapple trees, bottled, curded, jammed and jellied accordingly.

I have roasted longhorn cattle and succulent, snowy fatted Middle White pig at home in Somerset; *maiale al latte* and porchetta in Tuscany and Piemonte.

I have caught spiny lobsters off Inis Turk in Ireland and eaten brown trout from Doo Lough. I have ventured snake and snake wine in Hong Kong, though I drew the line at the blood being squeezed into a bowl after the snake's head had been chopped off for 'potency and stamina'. Said with a knowing wink.

I have poached the first wild sea trout to swim up the rivers Dart and Tamar in spring and picked warm cherries from orchards high in the Luberon hills in early summer.

But Robert Frost's poem 'The Road Not Taken' probably sums up best where I stand now, looking out across life's hilly climb in search of a new, or rediscovered, landscape for the eye and the heart.

The road less travelled has always been the one that has lured me, though I have often fallen off it for not quite daring to stay its course. We are led astray and against our better instincts, we rush down ravines without always sensing danger or impasse. As in our cooking lives, we learn most from going off-road if we pay attention and understand, try to make sense of these unexplored, un-signposted corners we were drawn to.

I would no longer choose the king of the river fish, sea trout, or tender, pale Italian veal if I was forced to choose a singular luxury.

Last summer I boarded my friend John K's boat off Old Head in County Mayo, the great horseshoe of Clew Bay edged with lavender mountains as we chugged out to sea. We left the bay and its calm waters for the open sea. No pitching and rolling, no white horses, the swell was a gently rhythmed undulation.

The west of Ireland coast that I look out over from my summer house is a landscape I always see afresh and am invigorated by. The strands are long, silver-white emptinesses and when the wind blows, the grains of sand whip across them like a desert storm. Nature is wilder, more dangerous, more exposed and exposing here. The horizon is abbreviated by a few little islands that we sail to, Clare, Inis Turk, Inis Bofin, then it is open sea all the way to America.

It was a clear blue day with everything reflecting and reflected in everything else, sun, cloud, blue sky on water, mountain, light.

Julia had her three children on board, I had my younger daughter, Charissa; Merci, John K's wife, one of my oldest friends, was with us. We didn't go too far out to the choppier waters of the open sea; we followed the coastline's contour and let the boat drift, let out our lines and waited.

There is something about the slapping of water on wood, the gentle rock and sway, the communion as you look down into the indigo depths, the sea salt and sun on skin, the jigging of a line with five or six feathered hooks on it that stops time in its tracks. It stops all sense of urgency and fret and disproportion. You are subservient to the task, the sea, the fish.

A shoal arrived and suddenly we were all reeling in like it was a lottery: more, faster, large, small, petrolly sea-blue-green mackerel with their herringbone black stripes and silver underbellies.

I knocked them on the head as fast as John unhooked each line. The children screamed with pleasure and excitement. I gutted and soaked the fish in a bucket I'd thrown out on a rope and hauled up slopping with chill seawater. My hands reeked of fish blood, I was spattered all over. No matter. My skin and jeans stuck with sequins of fish scales, my face rimed with salt spray.

When we had caught as many silver darting devils as we thought we could eat, and extra for all our neighbours, we stopped.

Don't take advantage of nature and never, ever waste it.

I lit the primus in the tiny sheltered wheelhouse.

I placed whole fish on the black grill and watched as the blue flames spat and leapt at them, charring their skin to uneven crispness and forcing their oily flesh to release its yellow liquid into the tinfoil below.

I flipped the fish over, watching the eyes sadden glaucomically as they cooked to a trembling white. Merci and I laid out homemade brown bread, dark with blackstrap molasses and thickly spread salty butter and cut lemons.

I splayed the fish out onto a plate, pulling the rakes of spine away from the flesh.

We dabbed hot sweet flesh onto bread and poured over the oily juices. An omega ocean of goodness.

There is no luxury like poverty.

There is no more luxury than the bounty of the sea and of catching it for yourself and your family.

Day-old mackerel isn't even the same fish, the flesh dulls, the silver tarnishes, the oil begins to lose its life and go rancid.

There is no fish like a poor man's fish caught and eaten in an Atlantic breeze with those you love and it takes the practice of luxury to shy you away from it.

I would catch mackerel here from the quay with my brother Dan or out on my friend Alec's lobster potting boat, *Eileen*, all August and sell them for a penny a piece when we were children. I felt rich and brave and special.

I feel rich and brave and special again.

The gulls wheel and snap behind the boat as we chuck heads and spines overboard.

The fish we're taking home trail in netted bags through the water as we motor back to Old Head pier.

There is nothing finer.

MARTIN YAN is the host of the Yan Can Cook television show, author of more than 30 cookbooks and the Chef/Partner of M.Y. China restaurant in San Francisco. When he isn't traveling the world, he is tending his garden and koi pond at his Bay Area home.

IN MY MOTHER'S KITCHEN

Martin Yan

Through my travel and participations in food events all over the world, I have been privileged to meet with many famous culinary icons and talented cooking professionals. Not surprising, our conversations often gravitate toward the topic of food, namely, how we all got started, and what were some of those pivotal moments in our careers. To be honest, I have been quite envious of some of the stories I'd heard. Apparently quite a number of my colleagues received their epiphany in some of the most exotic locales in the world, and under the most charming sets of circumstances.

Me? I had my moment, my earliest moment anyway, on a bare floor, under a rickety kitchen table. I was four years old and the spot under our kitchen table was my private sanctuary.

Home was a humble two-room house on the edge of the Southern Chinese city of Guangzhou. Of course this was a million years ago so Guangzhou was not quite the industrial juggernaut that it is today. Back then it was more rural than urban, and our house sat alongside a winding canal, with a muddy path lying outside our front door, paving the way to civilization.

From my domain under the table I could survey our entire kitchen, which was nothing more than a four-foot by six alcove. The 'stove' was a single wood-burning contraption; on top sat a huge (at least to the eyes of a four year old) cast iron wok. It was black and shiny like a lacquered tray. My mother was the chief cook, domestic goddess and number one dish washer, and being a family of simple means, we weren't exactly well-stocked in the utensils department. Luckily, my mother was gifted and skilled, and she made the best out of what we had: an all-purpose cleaver, a bamboo steamer, and the most basic sets of pots and bowls. Years later I would make jokes about those days. We were too poor to afford shelves. Funny yes, but true nevertheless.

One thing about our style of 'country' living, we were fairly self-sufficient when it came to food. This means that we actually grew most of what we consumed. You can say that we never had any food that was out of season. If it wasn't in season, we didn't have it in our little garden and on our rickety table at supper. Everything was fresh, naturally fresh, since we didn't have a refrigerator. It is ironic that in today's high-tech society the average family, with all the advance gadgets, is struggling more to eat fresh and healthy food. Perhaps they need to take a lesson from us poor folks back in rural China.

Back to the kitchen table and my special 'ah-ha' moment.

Up until that point, my relation with food was, shall we say, all 'above the table', as in what was on the plates my mother had prepared for supper. My younger brother and I were treated to mostly traditional Cantonese food—mildly seasoned, light and clean sauces, steamed dishes, lots of rice, and most importantly an abundance of fresh fruits and vegetables. Unlike the moms in the West, ours never had to tell us to clean our plates (or bowls), or tell us to remember the starving children elsewhere. Sitting in front of our nightly feast we would waste little time gobbling up everything. Afterwards we would lick our little chopsticks and wonder what was for dinner the following night. Little did we worry, or wonder, how our mother managed to make all those delicious dishes in that tiny kitchen of ours.

Then one day I crawled underneath our table, and everything changed.

My mother was a tiny woman, never reached five feet in height. She was, in today's language, a single mom, being widowed at an early age. Imagine her life back in those days, and with two toddlers to provide for, to make sure that they eat properly every day. It must have been a real struggle. Yet, those who knew my mother would all tell you that she was the most positive woman anyone would ever meet. She was the prime example of self-reliance. 'Do it yourself,' she would tell us, 'Nobody is going to do it for you!' Whatever 'it' was, she certainly set a fine example, and my brother and I have followed that our entire lives.

She never received any formal training as a cook. Everything she did she learned on her own, by her intuition and keen observation of others. She was a quick learner and I am privileged to have inherited that wonderful gift from her.

Back in those days professional chefs (more commonly referred to as those who cooked for a living) took their profession less for love and passion for cooking and more for opportunity and necessity. My mother became a cook, first in her own tiny restaurant, and later, after the Communist takeover, in a government-run eatery. Back then, you did what you needed to do to survive, especially when you were a widow with two sons.

Watching my mother in action in our own small kitchen had transformed me, her four year old son, from a pint-sized foodie to one who aspired to, one day, do all that chopping, stirring, steaming, and fussing over pots of winter melon soups and stews of tasty beef tendons. I wanted to do the magic that she did, taking a few basic ingredients and in no time transforming them into dishes that my brother and I would pine for day after day.

From beneath the kitchen table I could more than see what my mother was doing, I could also hear all that wonderful sounds, of her scraping the large wok, stirring the various pots, chopping on the old wooden chopping block. I learned most of my knife-cutting skills while I was an apprentice in a Hong Kong restaurant but I was first inspired by the 'chop chop chop' of my mom's cleaver.

But more than the sound I could also smell the wonderful aroma as each dish she was making was nearing its completion. I could smell the fresh garlic and ginger in the wok, then the browning of stocks of long beans and green onion, then the sweet smell of dark soy. On special occasions my mother would steam pork and duck sausages in the rice pot, and that incredible aroma would permeate not just the kitchen but the entire house and my nose and mouth would be watering the entire time.

To this day, whenever I came across that same wonderful smell of sausages steaming over plain white rice, I would always think of home. And I would be four years old all over again. Indeed, I would trade that precious spot underneath our wobbly kitchen table for any exotic destination far, far away. It was from that very spot that I first opened my eyes, ears and nose to the world of culinary art. There was where a four-year-old boy would one day emerge, taking the advice from his mother, to do things for himself because nobody else would do it for him. To take that muddy path that laid outside the two-room house, and to begin his culinary journey of a lifetime.

MICHAEL POLLAN is the author of seven books, including *The Omnivore's Dilemma* and, most recently, *Cooked: A Natural History of Transformation*.

MADE BY HAND
Michael Pollan

A couple of years ago, I traveled to Seoul to learn all I could about kimchi and how to make it. I was doing research on fermented foods for my book *Cooked*, and my education had already taken me to Iceland to sample hakarl (shark that has been buried for weeks—nasty) and to Shanghai for the accurately named stinky tofu. Fermented foods are often strongly—okay, offputtingly—flavored and often prized for that very reason. The Chinese relish their stinky tofu—blocks of tofu steeped for weeks in a slurry of rotten vegetables—but regard a washed-rind cheese with disgust. Sandor Katz, the great fermento and one of my mentors in the smellier culinary arts, has put the matter memorably: 'Between fresh and rotten there is a creative space where some of the most compelling flavors arise.'

Indeed. This is precisely what we mean by an 'acquired taste', and in Seoul I got to observe the process of acquisition in action. In Seoul I visited the kimchi museum on the south side of town: one of two kimchi museums in Seoul, I learned, and six in the country. Kimchi is a national dish of which Koreans are justly proud, but six museums dedicated to fermented cabbage seemed like a lot. At the museum I visited, I spent a morning watching class after class of kindergarteners troop through the displays, each uniformed child carrying an identical yellow backpack. The children studied dioramas depicting women rubbing bright red paste into cabbage leaves, passed by tableaux of ancient urns, cases with plastic peppers of every size and shade of red, piles of spice, etc. The children were well behaved but clearly bored, so I asked a docent why a field trip to a kimchi museum was part of the kindergarten curriculum. She replied with the sort of measured patience one reserves for a visitor exhibiting an inability to grasp the obvious.

'Children are not born liking kimchi.'

They have to learn. Why? Because an acquired taste like the one for kimchi is how cultures help knit themselves together. *We are the people who like this stuff.* Easy and universal tastes—for sweet things, for example—will never help delineate a culture in the way a polarizing food can. The taste of fermented foods is, I came to understand, the taste of us and them.

That is the first thing I learned in Seoul, and this was the thing I came there expecting to learn. But the wonder of reporting is always the thing you don't come expecting to learn, the lessons not on the syllabus. In the course of researching *Cooked*, I worked with many memorable cooking teachers, but in some ways the most memorable was Hyeon Hee Lee, a Korean woman who worked with the local Slow Food chapter, and had offered to teach me how to make traditional kimchi in a village an hour's drive outside of Seoul. It was a fairly brief encounter, no more than a few hours, but in retrospect it did as much as any other to help me understand what cooking was all about, or could be, in the right hands.

Before we began, Hyeon Hee made sure, through our translator, that I understood that there are a hundred different ways of making kimchi; what she was going to teach me was just one way, the way of her mother and grandmother before that.

Hyeon Hee had done most of the prep before I arrived, brining the Napa cabbages overnight and pounding the red peppers, garlic and ginger into a thick paste. What remained was for us to carefully rub the brilliant red paste into the leaves of the cabbages, which remain intact, one leaf at a time. The process was painstaking, almost absurdly so. You had to make sure that every internal and external square inch of every leaf of every head of cabbage received its own spice massage. Then you folded the leaves back on themselves and wrapped them around so that the whole thing vaguely resembled a pretzel, before gently placing the bright-scarlet knot at the bottom of an urn. Once the urn was full, it would be buried outside in the earth, beneath a little lean-to in the backyard.

333

While we worked together through that wintry November afternoon, kneeling side by side on straw mats, Hyeon Hee mentioned that Koreans traditionally made a distinction between the 'tongue taste' and the 'hand taste' of a food. *Hand taste?* I was beginning to have my doubts about the translator. But as Hyeon Hee elaborated on the distinction, while the two of us gently and methodically massaged spice into leaf, the distinction began to come into a rough focus.

Tongue taste is the straightforward chemical interaction that occurs whenever certain molecules make contact with tastebuds on the tongue, something that happens with all foods as a matter of course. Tongue taste is the kind of easy, accessible flavor that any food scientist or manufacturer can reliably produce in order to make food appealing. 'McDonald's has tongue taste,' Hyeon Hee explained.

Hand taste, however, involves something much greater than mere flavor. It is the infinitely more complex experience of a food that bears the unmistakable signature of the individual who made it—the care and thought and idiosyncrasy that that person has put into the work of preparing it. Hand taste cannot be simulated, Hyeon Hee insisted, and hand taste is the reason we go to all this trouble, massaging the individual leaves of each cabbage, and then folding them and packing them in the urn just so. What hand taste is, I understood all at once, is the taste of love— immediately recognizable, and impossible to fake.